BREAKING BOUNDARIES
THE MORE WE KNOW, THE MORE WE GROW

DR. KIM SPIVEY-HUNTER

Vision Publishing House
support@vision-publishinghouse.com
www.vision-publishinghouse.com

ISBN: 978-1-955297-57-8

LCCN: 2024903533

VISION PUBLISHING
H O U S E

To my family, who has encouraged me to continue reading, studying, writing, and asking tough questions...

Striving for excellence motivates you;
striving for perfection is demoralizing.

—Harriet B. Braiker

CONTENTS

Introduction

Metaphysics is a term that would rarely be considered when addressing a person's "life of faith." To many, these are two totally different aspects of existence and are therefore unrelated. Then, to propose for consideration the notion that metaphysics can actually be used or abused to influence one's life of faith is an event further stretched in an individual's imagination. Let's be reminded that metaphysics is the branch of philosophy that examines the fundamental nature of reality, including the relationship between mind and matter, between substance and attribute, and between potentiality and actuality.

In full transparency, I did consider this very notion many years ago and sought a deeper understanding, asking questions of family, friends, and clergy. Unfortunately, my inquiries were met with either partial answers, no answers, or, worst of all, belittling comments. It appeared to have been perceived that my questions were intended to question others' faith or beliefs, or better yet, to expose some form of charlatanic practices. As I was very new in my Christian walk, I backed off, never fully accepting any of the responses in my quest to understand the unexplainable.

When completing my first doctoral degree, my initial concerns came rushing back like a mighty wind, with the intent to desolate all that I had achieved in my faith walk. Questions began to spring up that had never been answered but were buried to maintain peace and protect the status quo. It was from that research and study that this topic now needs not only to be further investigated but also to establish some form of tangible resolution, something that I can sink my teeth into.

With that, the notion of charlatanic practices also came back to light. It is only befitting that a deeper analytical inspection of metaphysical manipulation's impact on people's faith be conducted. In this, it has to be made clear that my approach will be in the form of skepticism. This is to simply inform the reader that the question of "Has metaphysical manipulation impacted people's faith?" will be looked at from three ongoing and entwining perspectives, blending the past, present, and future. I was not aware that skepticism is not a bad thing or a "doomsday" crier but simply questions.

"Quick to question and slow to believe."

—Pyrrho of Elis

The above quote is now my current practice in reasoning. There are those who may feel challenged by this, and that is fine for them. As for me, judgment will be withheld until my questions have been satisfied.

This particular topic has been looked at by some very reputable and intriguing individuals. There is "Groundwork for the Metaphysics of Morals" and "Ethical Philosophy: Grounding for the Metaphysics of Morals and Metaphysical Principles of Virtue" by Immanuel Kant. There's a text authored by Matthew Kelly entitled "The Biggest Lie in the History of Christianity: How the Modern Culture Is Robbing Billions of People of Happiness." Additionally, there are other books like "Philosophy of Religion: Thinking about Faith," authored by C. Stephen Evans, and a host of other articles and reports on this very topic.

Throughout this book, I will focus attention on seven questions that I should be able to provide some insight on. The questions are as follows:

1. What is metaphysics?
2. What is faith?
3. What is the correlation between metaphysics and faith?
4. Are metaphysics, faith, and religion connected?

5. How does the relationship between metaphysics and religion impact faith?
6. Has there been a breach in the trust placed in faith-based leadership or organized religion?
7. Where do we go from here?

CHAPTER 1

Has Metaphysical Manipulation Impacted People's Faith?

Is there any point in public debate in a society where hardly anyone has been taught how to think, while millions have been taught what to think?

—Peter Hitchens

This is the question that I will be examining and sharing insights on with you. The purpose of this book is not to persuade anyone to abandon their faith journey. Instead, it aims to initiate a broader discussion around the question: "Is the Christian Church abusing metaphysics to create a false reality and labeling it as a life of faith?" Before we delve into this exploration, it is essential to clarify some general but specific terms that will be frequently referenced.

The rationale behind establishing agreed-upon definitions and explanations of terms is to ensure that readers interpret the information from the author's perspective, not their own. These terms will be consistently used throughout the book, so establishing a set of reasonable definitions is crucial.

Metaphysics, as defined by Wikipedia, is "the branch of philosophy that examines the fundamental nature of reality, including the relationship between mind and matter, between substance and attribute, and between potentiality and actuality." The next term to consider is manipulation. Manipulation is a fascinating term because every defining source seems to use the term to define itself. To gain a clearer understanding, let's first look at the term 'manipulate.' According to Oxford Languages, to manipulate is "to control or influence (a person or situation) cleverly, unfairly, or unscrupulously." The same source defines manipulation as "the action of manipulating someone in a clever or unscrupulous way." Generally speaking, 'manipulate' may refer to a one-time action, while 'manipulation' suggests ongoing and continuous behavior. Additionally, there is psychological manipulation, which is a type of social influence aiming to change the behavior or perception of others through indirect, deceptive, or underhanded tactics. Such methods, which advance the interests of the manipulator often at the expense of others, can be viewed as exploitative and devious.

The term 'faith' also warrants examination and is understood in two contexts, both as nouns: one being "complete trust or confidence in someone or something," and the other as "a strong belief in God or in the doctrines of a religion, based on spiritual apprehension rather than proof," according to Oxford Languages.

"Impacted' is defined as being strongly affected by something. Lastly, we will address the term 'people.' While it might seem straightforward, it is crucial to remember that in this context, 'people' does not refer to an individual but to a group considered as a whole, such as an ethnic group, nation, or the public of a polity.

Returning to the original question: has metaphysical manipulation impacted people's faith? The answer varies widely, from yes to no, based on a plethora of scholarly texts, journal articles, and surveys, each providing various justifiable reasons and perspectives.

CHAPTER 2

A Deeper Look at Metaphysics

The unexamined life is not worth living.

—Socrates

Metaphysics is the branch of philosophy that deals with the first principles of things, including abstract concepts such as being, knowing, substance, cause, identity, time, and space. According to the book of Oxford Languages, "They would regard the question of the initial conditions for the universe as belonging to the realm of metaphysics or religion." However, when we consult Wikipedia, it states, "Metaphysics is the branch of philosophy that examines the fundamental nature of reality, including the relationship between mind and matter, between substance and attribute, and between potentiality and actuality." To consider another resource, the Stanford Encyclopedia of Philosophy offers a definition or explanation of metaphysics, with the very first line reading, "It is not easy to say what metaphysics is. Ancient and medieval philosophers might have said that metaphysics was, like chemistry or astrology, to be defined by its subject matter: metaphysics was the 'science' that studied 'being as such' or 'the first causes of things'

3

or 'things that do not change.'" Like with most philosophical concepts and discourses, there is a tendency to engage in what has been termed infinite regress.

Infinite regress is at the heart of Thomas Aquinas's cosmological argument for the existence of God. The term simply means that ideas, concepts, or beliefs build upon other ideas, concepts, or beliefs, with no identifiable beginning. To sum up infinite regression in a light-hearted manner, one might ponder, which came first, the chicken or the egg?

We will revisit Sir Thomas Aquinas later in the text, but for now, let's establish a more accessible understanding of metaphysics. Metaphysics is believed to have originated from the Greek term meta ta physika, meaning "after the things of nature" or "beyond what is physical." Within this framework lies the distinction between realism and idealism.

With metaphysical idealism, individuals tend to create a reality based on their thoughts, contrasting with metaphysical realism, which perceives reality as existing independently of one's thoughts. This concept might seem abstract, but consider the philosopher René Descartes, famous for his assertion, "I think, therefore I am." From this viewpoint, because he thought he existed, then he indeed existed. This perspective is quite different from that of John Locke, a philosopher grounded in realism, who believed that knowledge comes through our senses and experiential learning.

We must not dwell too long on the realism or idealism of metaphysics, as neither perspective is without its faults. In modern times, a more widely accepted definition of metaphysics is that it "refers to the study of what cannot be reached through objective studies of material reality." This explanation does not end here. Metaphysical studies are typically divided into three categories:

1. ontology or general
2. epistemology
3. cosmology or religion

While cosmology and religion have often been treated as separate disciplines, for the continuity of thought in this book, we may consider them together. Just as we explored René Descartes and John Locke to understand the metaphysical arguments around realism and idealism, we will also highlight three individuals who led the discussions on the ontological, epistemological, and cosmological arguments in metaphysics. The goal is to establish a clear understanding of metaphysics to further determine if metaphysical manipulation impacts people's faith.

Ontological

It is beneficial to start with the understanding that 'ontological' is a term of Greek and Latin origins. Its etymological foundation might be confused by some with 'taxonomy,' as both terms pertain to the study of entities. However, while taxonomy seeks to establish a hierarchy, ontology delves into the nature of being and existence. Ontology examines levels of truth, realism, power, and other conceptually relevant ideas, exploring their interrelations and whether they affirm, challenge, or negate each other's existence in levels or totality.

An effort to prove God's existence, the ontological argument, uses a form of reasoning that might seem inverse. Ontologists propose that one can deduce the existence of God according to God's definition. Saint Anselm, a Christian philosopher and Benedictine monk, is noteworthy here. He viewed theology as "faith seeking understanding," not questioning God's existence but aiming to demonstrate that God exists both conceptually and in reality.

"If therefore that than which nothing greater can be conceived exists in the understanding alone, then this thing than which nothing greater can be conceived is something than which a greater can be conceived. And this is clearly impossible. Therefore, there can

be no doubt at all that something than which a greater cannot
be conceived exists in both the understanding and in reality."

—Saint Anselm (1033–1109)
Proslogion

The primary ontological argument comes from Saint Anselm of Canterbury. He proposed the thought that there must be a being that is greater than any other being, and that being "is God." When reading about Saint Anselm's thoughts and criticisms, one famous philosopher who built upon his works was none other than René Descartes, the seventeenth-century French philosopher. Descartes is widely known for his famous quote, "I think therefore I am." His philosophical positioning was that in order to understand and believe in something, one should shed their current beliefs and seek to establish a belief based on tangible evidence.

In addition, Pascal adds his perspective by saying, "It is incomprehensible that God should exist, and it is incomprehensible that He should not exist" (Pascal). For this reason, one can conclude that God is so great and perfect that we cannot conceive; therefore, there must be a God

Epistemological

The term 'epistemology' was coined by James Frederick Ferrier, a Scottish philosopher, to denote the theory of knowledge. Britannica defines epistemology as: "the philosophical study of the nature, origin, and limits of human knowledge." Essential epistemological questions include:

1. What is knowledge?
2. How does one know what they know?
3. How does one acquire knowledge?
4. How does knowledge begin?

One reason that epistemology and epistemological conceptual systems are even considered is best explained in William B. Badke's idea shared in his book, "Teaching Research Processes," published in 2012.

Check the text in the chapter "The Role of Disciplinary Thinking in Research Processes," under the section "Philosophy: Epistemology of information." 'Epistemology' is a philosophical concept that considers the nature of the sources of information we value. It asks questions like these: Where does our disciplinary information come from? What forms does it take? Why is such information seen as significant to our discipline? How do we determine what sources are reliable/valuable and what are not?"

The actual concept that would lead one to question the origin of what they believe and its validity is essential to the metaphysical discourse.

Cosmological / Religious

The term 'cosmological' currently has what is called a cosmological principle. The cosmological principle is based on the following thoughts.

> "The assumptions that are made about our universe include that
> it is isotropic and homogeneous. 'Isotropic' means the universe
> looks approximately the same in all directions. 'Homogenous'
> means one large region of the universe is approximately
> the same as any other large region of the universe."
>
> —The Cosmological Principle

Thomas Aquinas, an Italian philosopher and theologian from the thirteenth century, sought to provide evidence for the existence of God. He did this by establishing (not actually with any tangible evidence) five proof points, which are degrees, causation, motion, contingency, and the teleological argument. A brief examination of each of the five proof points are shared below.

1. **Degrees** – This references the fact that the only way things can be measured or given a value is if they are compared to something perfect, and according to Thomas Aquinas, God is perfect.
2. **First Cause (Causation)** - There must be something/someone to "cause" things to happen. There could be no effect without a cause; therefore, the primary cause is God.
3. **Prime Mover (Motion)** - Things are always moving, and this movement must be caused by movers, which cause motion. He believed that the only way this could happen is if there was something moving the movers to begin with, and that prime mover must be God.
4. **Necessary Being (Contingency)** - With this part of the "proof" presented, Aquinas explained that things are based on other things. With that, there had to be something that was unchanging to establish the basis of everything else. The conclusion is that God is the one constant, never changing.
5. **Teleological Argument** - This concept states that the world is created so effectively that only a supreme being could have created it, and that being is God.

For a oneness of definition, as this text reads, metaphysics will be 'understood' as follows: "a branch of philosophy seeking to identify, qualify, and/or explain reality's existence from three conflicting perspectives: ontology, cosmology, and epistemology."

To gain a better perspective concerning metaphysics, it is only reasonable to review the works of some frequently referenced metaphysicians like Parmenides, Plato, Aristotle, Plotinus, Duns Scotus, Thomas Aquinas, Francisco Suarez, Nicolas Malebranche, Kant, Bertrand Russell, William Lame Craig, and so many others. Clearly, within the scope of this text, it would not be advantageous to review all the individual metaphysicians known. Nevertheless, as 'metaphysical manipulation' is at the core of this research, it is essential that primary metaphysical perspectives are introduced beginning with its founding philosophical fathers.

CHAPTER 3

The Relationship Between Metaphysics and Ontology

I do not feel obliged to believe that the same God who has endowed us with sense, reason, and intellect has intended us to forgo their use.

—Galileo Galilei

In this section of the text, we will take a more direct and succinct look at the relationship between metaphysics and ontology. Ontology primarily examines the nature of "being" or how things interrelate. It is a subdivision of metaphysics, which, as previously described, focuses on the first principles of things and their origins.

To gain insight into the basic foundations of ontology, it is essential to introduce Pythagoras, considered a founding philosopher in this field. His significance extends beyond his contributions to ontology, as Pythagoras is also recognized as a religious mystic, mathematician, and scientist. These facets of his identity are crucial for understanding the interplay between science, spirituality, faith, and religion within his philosophical framework.

As Larry Bell notably mentioned in his 2019 article, "Mystics of Major Historical Importance,"

> *All mystics have one thing in common: they attempt to make contact with the afterlife, the dead, or with their personal concept of God. It is common for notable mystics in history to begin their spiritual journey in a mainstream faith tradition, only to start their own movement after having major revelations.*

Like this quote from Larry Bell, Pythagoras had a following because he began to question the powers that be. Pythagoras actually taught that when the body dies, the soul does not.

Pythagoras studied under the temple priests in Egypt and a large number of other wise men. It was in Egypt that he gained his priesthood status. Many sources indicate that Pythagoras studied under the famed Egyptian priest Oenuphis of Heliopolis, which is believed to be what in fact led to his popularity (some liking him and others disliking him). Throughout his life, as he traveled from place to place, he would always establish a following. A few of his greatest students were his wife Theano and daughters Damo, Myia, and Arignote, which was an absolutely radical concept during those times. It is commonly shared that Pythagoras's wife, Theano, was a philosopher and leader within the school founded by Pythagoras, so much so that she continued the school after his death, as she was also a very well-respected Pythagorean philosopher.

Pythagoras believed in the idea that it was the opposite that established one's understanding of a concept. There could not be good without bad or hot without cold, or as Pythagoras put it, "If there is light, then there is darkness; if cold, heat; if height, depth; if solid, fluid; if hard, soft; if rough, smooth; if calm, tempest; if prosperity, adversity; if life, death." This leads to the relational ties between metaphysics and ontology. It would stand to reason that a temple priest would consider God in the realm of his understanding and belief systems.

The Stanford Encyclopedia of Philosophy notes, "Pythagoras succeeded in promulgating a new, more optimistic view of the fate of the soul after death and in founding a way of life that attracted many followers with its rigor and discipline."

In contemporary research and discourse, four primary points of interest emerge regarding Pythagoras's beliefs, listed without any specific order of importance or influence:

1. He founded a belief system in which his followers had very rigid dietary practices, self-discipline, and religious rituals.
2. He was very well-known because of his theories and beliefs concerning the soul, reincarnation, and the afterlife.
3. He was very well-versed in religious rituals and practices.
4. The belief that he had superhuman capabilities, or as Heraclitus described Pythagoras, "the chief of the charlatans."

As much of a scientist as Pythagoras was, there seems to be no credible evidence suggesting that he endeavored to prove the existence of God. This aspect of his belief system was seemingly taken for granted, reflecting a stance that aligns with a priori-based knowledge. A priori knowledge, as defined by the Routledge Encyclopedia of Philosophy, is:

an important term in epistemology since the seventeenth century, "a priori" typically connotes a kind of knowledge or justification that does not depend on evidence, or justification, from sensory experience. Talk of a priori truth is ordinarily shorthand for talk of truth knowable or justifiable independently of evidence from sensory experience; and talk of a priori concepts is usually talk of concepts that can be understood independently of reference to sensory experience.

Pythagoras based all his knowledge on theoretical deductions rather than actual observable or experienced data. Pythagoras was not the only philosopher reviewed who had strong ontological beliefs. Another individual who was of interest concerning ontology and metaphysics is David Hume. He has a totally different perspective concerning ontology and metaphysics. Whereas Pythagoras operated under the premise that they are almost one in the same and that everything begins with God, David Hume believed differently.

Looking at historical figures in their debates concerning ontology and its metaphysical impacts on human existence is seen as a topic of great and impassioned writings. If one was to consider David Hume, the Scottish philosopher, then one would conclude that an ontological argument has no substance as this type of argument is just not possible. David Hume was of the mindset that using a priori reasoning in isolation could prove nothing. He was insistent on posterior knowledge. Below is a definition of posterior knowledge as explained in the Routledge Encyclopedia of Philosophy:

> *"A posteriori" signifies a kind of knowledge or justification that depends on evidence, or warrant, from sensory experience. A posteriori truth is truth that cannot be known or justified independently of evidence from sensory experience, and posteriori concepts are concepts that cannot be understood independently of reference to sensory experience.*

Hume reached his physiological position according to his perception of knowledge acquisition. He was adamant that the way humans understand things is based on a combination of what we think and our feelings or emotions in combination with our senses. It is his assertion that our beliefs about things are influenced based on what we see and what we can physically experience.

In his writing, Hume refers to these two experiences combined as perceptions, again based on what we can see and hear. In one of his writings, *A Treatise of Human Nature (1739–1740)*, he explained that "impressions are felt, and ideas are thoughts," and because of these, humans must experience both to gain understanding or knowledge of something.

One of the philosophical movements called logical positivism was born due to David Hume's conjectures: "Logical positivism—this *theory of knowledge* asserted that only statements verifiable through direct observation or *logical proof* are meaningful in terms of conveying truth value, information or factual content" (Wikipedia). In other words, one should not believe anything to be true if its truth cannot be validated.

We must remember that David Hume is more famously known for his "is-ought problem." For clarity of understanding, a definition/description is shared below:

The 'is-ought problem,' as articulated by the Scottish philosopher and historian David Hume, arises when one makes claims about what ought to be that are based solely on statements about what is. Hume found that there seems to be a significant difference between positive statements (about what is) and prescriptive or normative statements (about what ought to be), and that it is not obvious how one can coherently move from descriptive statements to prescriptive ones. 'Hume's law' or 'Hume's guillotine' is the thesis that, if a reasoner only has access to non-moral and non-evaluative factual premises, the reasoner cannot logically infer the truth of moral statements.

—Wikipedia

This distinction initially seemed pretty obvious to me living in this century, in which we understand that "is" stands for something that has been affirmed, and "ought" stands for something that 'should have been' affirmed. In general, we have a conceptual understanding, but with the support of dictionary.com, the definitions are shared. 'Is' stands for the third person singular present, indicative of be (dictionary.com), and 'ought' stands for an 'auxiliary verb' (used to express duty or moral obligation).

Examples include:

Every citizen ought to help. (In this example, *ought* is used to express justice, moral rightness, or the like.)

He ought to be punished. You ought to be ashamed. (Here, the term is used to express propriety, appropriateness, etc.)

You ought to be home early. We ought to bring her some flowers. (Here, *ought* is used to express probability or natural consequence.)

This insertion may seem trivial, but it is not as this distinction reflects the very crux of Hume's thoughts as communicated so cleverly by Wikipedia's posting of "David Hume's skepticism," sharing a section from an article entitled "Is-Ought Problem," which reads,

> In <u>*A Treatise of Human Nature*</u> *(1739),* <u>*David Hume*</u> *discusses the problems in grounding normative statements in positive statements, that is in deriving* <u>*ought from is*</u>*. It is generally regarded that Hume considered such derivations untenable, and his 'is–ought' problem is considered a principal question of* <u>*moral philosophy.*</u>
>
> *Hume shared a political viewpoint with early Enlightenment* <u>*philosophers*</u> *such as* <u>*Thomas Hobbes*</u> *(1588–1679) and* <u>*John Locke*</u> *(1632–1704). Specifically, Hume, at least to some extent, argued that religious and national hostilities that divided European society were based on unfounded beliefs. In effect, Hume contended that such hostilities are not found in* <u>*nature,*</u> *but are a human creation, depending on a particular time and place, and thus unworthy of mortal conflict.*

Reviewing the thoughts, beliefs, and conjectures of philosophical leaders of the past has its place in any form of viable research. As research continues and new evidence is presented, it is essential that newer concepts, thoughts, theories, and conjectures are at least reviewed and considered. With that, the name Harman Graham appeared in a few articles, and that provoked a need to identify who this individual is and what his contribution to the discussion about metaphysics and ontology actually are.

Graham Harman is currently a professor of philosophy in Egypt at the American University in Cairo. Graham Hartman's PhD was issued in 1999 at the DePaul University in Chicago. As a philosopher, he has focused his attention on ontology and metaphysics. One area that he is well-known for is speculative realism.

Speculative realism is not an easy term to define. It is better explained. 'Speculative' is when some thought, action, or concept is marked by questioning curiosity or when things are theoretical rather than demonstrable. 'Realism' is the attitude or practice of accepting a situation as it is and being prepared to deal with it accordingly. Combining these, speculative realism suggests a mindset where one might accept the reality of a situation as presented yet concurrently question the authenticity or validity of the information, even preparing for outcomes that differ from those suggested. This is a relatively new school of thought and has combined the worlds of art with metaphysics.

One relatively simple visualization is when a pencil is placed in a glass of water, the pencil appears as though it is in two parts. However, once the pencil is lifted from the glass, it is one whole pencil.

According to one article, it shared, "Harman's goal in philosophy has been to reject anthropocentric philosophical views in favor of a *metaphysical realist approach.*" Anthropocentric is regarding humankind as the central or most important element of existence, especially as opposed to God or animals. In Harman's view of the world, everything created and in existence is on a "level ontological and metaphysical plane." In Harman's philosophy, everything has its own basis of understanding and should not be viewed according to biased anthropocentric qualities. In other words, there does not have to be a good reason for one to understand that something is bad.

So good will be good according to the standards of good.

Another modern-day philosopher is John Heil, who is now considered one of the top fifty philosophers of our time. John Heil published several articles and books concerning ontology and the mind. A little background information on John Heil: his theories include a unique blending of mental philosophy with metaphysics. His works and current course offerings are taking a close look at metaphysics and one's mind and thought processes. He is a professor of philosophy currently employed at the Washington University in St. Louis. As the online source (IAI Academy) shares, John Heil asks these very thought-provoking questions and provides a statement as the introduction of a college course that he is currently teaching. It reads as follows: "Didn't science kill philosophy? Can metaphysics uncover the way the world is? Philosopher John Heil revives metaphysics and confronts the big questions of substance, causation, and consciousness."

It was also written that, "Heil considers how our 'notions' of causation and truth are making contributions to our ontological understanding of the world and pursues the application of this ontology to contemporary philosophical problems."

This is interesting, as Heil, in his philosophical sharing, is forcing individuals to reconsider what they are considering foundational truths to be and how these thoughts impact people. In one of his lectures, John Heil shares that in his opinion, philosophy is not in the head but in the heart, and that is what drives the thoughts. He is leading the notion of how we merge our experiences with what the world tells us things are to form an opinion or belief.

Showing this relationship could cause one to further inquire if the faith of many is impacted by metaphysic manipulation. Are people believing and having faith according to what they know for themselves or what they have heard? Is what people feel in their hearts or their understanding of the foundational literature as it is/was written, presented, and "proven" the driving force behind their faith? Is faith based on a priori or a posteriori knowledge or some combination of the two? Based on the information previously shared, the question remains: "Has metaphysic manipulation impacted people's faith?"

What was shared as a oneness of definition according to this text for metaphysics will be *understood* as, "A branch of philosophy seeking to identify, qualify and/or explain reality's existence from three conflicting perspectives, ontology, cosmology, and epistemology."

CHAPTER 4

The Impact of Metaphysics and Ontology on One's Faith Walk

With man, we find ourselves facing a differing ontological order—an ontological leap, we could say. But in posing such a great ontological discontinuity, are we not breaking up the physical continuity which seems to be the main line of research about evolution in the fields of physics and chemistry? An appreciation for the different fields of scholarship allows us to bring together two points of view which at first may seem irreconcilable....But the experience of metaphysical knowledge, of self-consciousness and self-awareness, of moral conscience, of liberty or aesthetic and religious experience—these must be analyzed through philosophical reflection, while theology seeks to clarify the ultimate meaning of the Creator's design.

—Pope John Paul II

The above statement was shared by Pope John Paul II in his message to the Pontifical Academy of Sciences back in September 22, 1996. The focus of the session was "the Origin of Life and Evolution." In this session, Pope John Paul II recommended a "frank dialogue between the church and sciences" (including philosophy).

This information was selected and shared as it shows that it is time to look at the relationship between sciences and beliefs. This is not some new phenomena; individuals have been seeking for ages to try and explain how the human race began, how the world was formed, and for what purpose was the earth formed and humans created or existed. Understanding that ontology is simply trying to answer questions that appear to be non complex as they relate to existence and the purpose behind that existence: 'the why.'

Metaphysics looks to address reality and our understanding of reality. Both metaphysics and ontology can be utilized when seeking to qualify and/or disqualify one's faith. More importantly, in this portion of text, we will not be discussing the question of "What is faith?" That has been reserved for a later time. In this portion of the text, we will be addressing the impacts of metaphysical and ontological knowledge and further the impact that this knowledge has on a person's exercising of their faith.

It appears the foundation premises of both metaphysics and ontology were not intended to dispel a belief system but to validate it. The problem seems to have occurred when no one philosopher was able to prove the people's beliefs of these times. There was always that unanswered question, a question whose sought-after answer was so compelling, it caused people to seek an answer or explanation of the unexplainable or unanswerable. As it is suggested by Pope John Paul II, there should be somewhat of an interconnectedness between the church and science.

I pause here, as it is essential to the reader that you understand many of the sources utilized lean toward either the Catholic Church or the Christian community. I am in no way limiting the depth of this discussion to these two faith subgroups. There will be utilization of generalities made as the greater scope of this text includes all people of all faith backgrounds and those who indicate that they have no faith. Nor is this section intended to serve as an indictment against or a banner for one faith over another.

While looking for information concerning ontology and metaphysics and its impact on faith, there was a portion of text in the book "The Big Question" that spoke about Carl Sagan. What is interesting here is that Carl Sagan was a scientist, more specifically an astronomer, who once stated, "Science is much more than a body of knowledge. It is a way of thinking. This is central to its success. Science *invites us* to let the facts in, even when they don't conform to our preconceptions. It counsels us to carry alternative hypotheses in our heads and see which ones best match the facts" (p. 53).

Ontology begs the question, is your faith rational or irrational? And metaphysics pushes you to consider, where does one's faith come from? Both questions can lead one to embark upon a journey seeking foundational truths to support or validate what they have faith in or why they do not have faith at all.

I presuppose that an understanding of metaphysics and ontology would have an impact on an individual's faith walk. This being because one would have to establish whether their belief is rational or irrational. Then they would have to try to seek out the beginning of their faith to

determine if what they believe is the beginning or if there is something else. Nothing should be taken for granted.

Science does limit itself to what can be observed and measured, quantified, and qualified. But do those established limits mean that there is nothing beyond the realm of scientific knowledge? As we know, scientific theories are ever evolving, proving, and disproving themselves, time and time again. So a revealing thought is that science is not as concrete or formable as one cares to believe.

In fact, the one thing that we do know for sure is that scientific theories are based on "man's" flawed sense of knowledge, which is made up of their experiences, backgrounds, foundational beliefs, cultural norms, traditional religious beliefs, and egos. So in other words, science is both biased and fallible. It is because this can be said about science, there is a more leveled discussion plateau between science, faith, and religion.

One school of thought around psychology states that the area of one's first experiential perception was that the view and sense of awe comes prior to cognition. We, then, wonder about what we viewed that caught our attention. In "The Big Question: Why We Can't Stop Talking about Science, Faith, and God," written by Alister McGrath, he shares, "That's why Thomas Aquinas is right when he declares that 'the cause of that at which we wonder is hidden from us,' causing us to yearn to make sense of this heart-stopping experience of awe we see as a gateway to significance."

The impact of understanding both metaphysics and ontology can have on one's faith walk would possibly be to have them consider the rationality or irrationality of faith. What are the foundational beginnings of that which they have faith in? It would be better to consider at this stage to establish a collective understanding of what faith is.

CHAPTER 5

What Is Faith?

Faith is taking the first step, even when you don't see the whole staircase.

—Martin Luther King Jr.

When addressing faith, the Christian community generally refers to the Bible and will confidently direct an individual to the book of Hebrews 11:1 (KJV), which reads,

Now faith is the substance of things hoped for,
the evidence of things not seen.

When looking at the quote taken from the late Rev. Dr. Martin Luther King Jr. in connection to the verse of scripture above, it appears to present an understandable and logical representation of faith: "One is hoping that when they take that first step, although they do not have the evidence to prove it, that the whole staircase will be there." Reading these two explanations would lead one to believe that in order to exercise faith, all that must be done is to do things blindly and hope for the best.

Another explanation that appeared to give a more applicable explanation of what faith is comes from C. H. Spurgeon. Charles Haddon Spurgeon lived from 1834 to 1892. He was a renowned Victorian,

Calvinistic, Baptist minister. He is known and respected internationally with his sermons written and studied in several different languages.

C. H. Spurgeon suggested that 'faith' is comprised of knowledge, belief, and trust. Via a review of his different materials, he implies that first there is knowledge, meaning a person must know about something before they can have faith in it. Then knowledge is followed by belief in what you know. Then after the person has both knowledge and belief, they need to then trust. It is the combination of all three operating systematically that is the defining factor of faith.

It seems that for Spurgeon, trusting and believing in what they have knowledge of is the definition of faith. To be fair, the knowledge that Spurgeon was referencing was the Bible and the belief in what is written, trusting that it is the truth.

If faith was that cut-and-dried, then there would be no basis for the question that has been posed for this research: "Has metaphysical manipulation impacted people's faith?" Well, as research would have it, faith is not so easily defined or understood. Looking at several different sources, it has been revealed that the word 'faith' has a few simulations with varying components. To view faith in a variety of aspects, we will utilize the King James Version of the Bible, the Stanford Encyclopedia of Philosophy, and the Student Bible Dictionary in addition to some articles.

The point of this section is to identify what is faith. It is not an attempt to challenge one belief system over another or to serve as an indictment as to what individuals should believe and how they should act.

When looking to define faith beyond that of the Christian doctrine, to be as unbiased as possible, the Merriam-Webster Online Dictionary provided the broadest source of information. It defined 'faith' in the following manner:

1a: allegiance to duty or a person: LOYALTY
Example: lost faith in the company's president

b (1): fidelity to one's promises

(2): sincerity of intentions
Example: acted in good faith

2 a (1): belief and trust in and loyalty to God
(2): belief in the traditional doctrines of a religion

B (1): firm belief in something for which there is no proof
Example: clinging to the faith that her missing son would one day return

(2): complete trust

3: something that is believed especially with strong conviction
especially: a system of religious beliefs

Example: The Protestant *faith*

on faith
: without question
Example: took everything he said *on faith*

Looking at the range of explanatory terms, they begin with allegiance, fidelity, and sincerity of intentions. The second set of defining terms are trust in, loyalty to, loyalty to God, and belief in the traditional doctrines of a religion. The defining terminology then shifts to the levels of belief and trust, to explain that the belief is firm in something for which there is no proof with complete trust and strong convictions without question. This definition reads to be all-inclusive, nonetheless, as the topic at hand is metaphysical manipulation. An explanation of the word 'faith' from a philosophical perspective would prove to be valuable for a correlative understanding. With that, the question "How does one account for their faith?" will be addressed via the view of philosophy.

CHAPTER 6

How Does One Account for Their Faith?

So we, being many, are one body in Christ, and every one members one of
another. Having then gifts differing according to the grace that is given to
us, whether prophecy, let us prophesy according to the proportion of faith.

—Romans 12:5–6 (KJV)

W hen considering faith, it would almost be considered negligent to presuppose that every individual person has the same level or type of faith. As there is not one tangible way to define this belief, that causes action—not only physical action in which they may act upon this faith, but also psychosocial emotion, whereas one's faith could cause psychological and physical distress. It is conceptually this very notion that requires a philosophical look at how individuals "account" for their faith.

The Stanford Encyclopedia of Philosophy takes the word 'faith' and analyzes it from ten different perspectives referenced as models. Each one will be fleetingly visited so as not to lose focus of the question, "How does one account for their faith?" The areas addressed are the affective component of faith, faith as knowledge, faith and reason (the epistemology of faith), faith as belief, faith as trust, faith as doxastic venture, faith as sub- or non- doxastic venture, faith and hope, faith as a virtue, and faith beyond orthodox theism.

The Affective Component of Faith

When considering one's *affective component of faith,* it is a sense of confidence and trust that is psychological in nature. According to J. S. Clegg (1979), this leads to what is referred to as an "overall default" attitude about life. It appears this component of faith is only based on what a person thinks about something. This is very different from the consideration of knowing about something. This could be indicative of the saying "Do not confuse me with the facts, I have my mind made up."

Faith as Knowledge

The next model, *faith as knowledge*, has a differing basis. This type of faith is associated with a cognitive thought process. Alvin Plantinga, an American philosopher, asks the questions, "What kind of knowledge is faith derived from? Is it knowledge 'by acquaintance' or 'propositional' knowledge 'by description' or both?" Mr. Plantinga follows the mindset of none other than John Calvin and shares this: "Calvin defines faith thus: 'a firm and certain knowledge of God's benevolence towards us, founded upon the truth of the freely given promise in Christ, both revealed to our minds and sealed upon our hearts through the Holy Spirit."

When considering what has been shared by Alvin Plantinga, faith as knowledge seems to be a sincere belief in what one feels and thinks as their knowledge base. With this form of faith, there is no *basis for logical or systematic thinking.*

Faith and Reason (The Epistemology of Faith)

However, when considering *faith and reason (the epistemology of faith)*, it seems clear to some that faith comes by way of reasoning, especially for theist philosophers. This may appear to be absolutely contradictory in thought and knowledge, but the philosopher Immanuel Kant is quoted as follows: "I have…found it necessary to deny knowledge, in order to make room for faith" (Critique of Pure Reason). This form of faith is based on the evidentialist principle. To clarify, a portion of the explanation taken from the Stanford Encyclopedia of Philosophy is shared here: "If faith consists in beliefs that have the status of knowledge, faith can hardly fail to be rational." If one has faith in God, then that faith is not without reason because the faith holder has reasoned that they can trust God because if God has done this for them, then God will do this for them as well.

Reflective Faith and the Question of Entitlement

When considering *reflective faith* and the *question of entitlement*, it is discovered that due to a person's thoughts about who they are or where they come from, they question if they are entitled to believe something. Another way to consider this type of faith is to do away with the theistic notion of faith altogether. This type of faith is always thinking, considering, and reflecting on what they have a confident expectation in and if they should. Although this can present as skepticism, this differs in that "from the perspective of reflective persons of faith (or would-be faith), the question of entitlement arises: are they rationally, epistemically—even, morally—entitled to adopt or continue in their faith?" (Stanford Encyclopedia of Philosophy). Overall, when considering this form of faith, what is key to understanding is that the person is reflecting and questioning their entitlement to having faith. Am I worthy?

Faith as Belief

With the *faith as a belief* model, many philosophical greats were considered, from Hume, Aquinas, Locke, and quite a few others. The notion of faith not being certain was the bedrock of the thought-provoking writings. This coincides with "the schoolboy's definition mentioned by William James: 'Faith is when you believe something that you know ain't true' (James 1896 [1956, 29])." In one portion of the text, the review of theist faith was mentioned and said to be made up of belief: "To have theist faith might thus be identified with holding a belief with theological content—that God exists, is benevolent towards us, has a plan of salvation, etc.—where this belief is also held with sufficient firmness and conviction." Richard Swinburne labeled this as the Thomist view (Stanford Encyclopedia of Philosophy). There was mention that this category of faith was considered and should be considered "factual hypotheses" because this faith is based on evidence, which, to some extent, supports the level of conviction. It was argued in the same article that the term 'factual hypotheses' invites the assumption that "theological convictions belong in the same category of factual claims as scientific theoretical hypotheses with which they accordingly compete."

Overall, faith as belief indicates that one's faith is not blind but based on a firmly held belief in something, which then allows them to trust the anticipated outcome. As for theistic faith, that would be the testimonials of the writers of the Bible. For theists, propositional truths are the foundation; either one believes, or they do not. Aquinas holds that faith is "midway between knowledge and opinion" (Summa Theologiae).

Faith as an Act of Trust

This model, *faith as an act of trust,* was interesting to review because initially, one would automatically state that faith equals trust. However, to better understand this model, a review on Wilfred Cantwell Smith is needed. He argues that "faith is not belief, but something of a quite different order," requiring "assent in the dynamic and personal sense of rallying to [what one takes to be the truth] with *delight and engagement*."

According to this model of faith, one must not only believe that God exists, but they have to believe in God and be willing to act on those beliefs. This model leans on the philosophical underpinnings of philosophers like J. L. Schellenberg and what he refers to as the operational model and McKaughan and Howard-Snyder. McKaughan and Howard-Snyder are referenced in the Encyclopedia of Philosophy because of their commitment to the understanding that faith in God will cause a faithfulness to God by virtue of actions.

When reading these philosophical outpourings, James 2:14 became a foundational truth for these individuals. James 2:14 reads, "What does it profit, my brethren, if someone says he has faith but does not have works?" McKaughan suggests that we should apply a more fiducial model to faith. With this model, one's faith is exercised as an action, a practical commitment not only as effective.

Due to this, the question has arrived considering whether when exercising faith as an act of trust, is it "blind faith" or "reasonable faith" in addition to "educational trust," "therapeutic trust," or "blind trust"? Again, as with so many areas of this book, I will stop here with Proverb 3:5 NIV: "Trust in the Lord with all your heart and lean not to your understanding." The fiducial model—a model of faith as trust—is understood not simply as an affective state (feeling of emotions or moods) but as an action.

Yet, as noted earlier, Aquinas also takes the ultimate object of faith to be God. "'The first reality,' and, furthermore, understands 'formed' faith as a trusting commitment to God, motivated by, and directed towards, love of God as one's true end" (Summa Theologiae).

When one takes it to be true in practical reasoning that someone will prove trustworthy, that mental act may be more or less epistemically rational; it would break the evidentialist norm to employ in a decision-theoretic calculation a credence that does not match one's available evidence.

Faith as Doxastic Venture

John Bishop shares, "A 'doxastic venture' model of faith—according to which having faith involves believing beyond what is rationally justifiable."

This model of faith is ideal for those who reject the model of theist faith as basic knowledge and who also think that the question of God's existence cannot be settled intellectually due to the available evidence. Faith as a doxastic venture allows those who trust already to venture beyond the available evidence. The doxastic venture on the basis of faith *accepts* that God exists and is true to the plan of salvation.

This belief in faith as a doxastic venture is further supported by William James. "James is thus able to explain the psychological possibility of doxastic venture: one already has a 'passionally' caused belief, which one then takes to be true in practical reasoning despite its lack of adequate evidential grounding" (Stanford Encyclopedia of Philosophy).

William James shared that faith is causally evoked. He notes that "a doxastic venture model of theistic faith reconciles faith as gift with faith's active components: taking a faith-proposition to be true in practical reasoning is a basic (mental) action (which leads on to further actions involved in trusting God and seeking to do God's will); the gift provides the motivational resources for this basic action, namely a firm belief in the truth of the faith-proposition, despite its lack of adequate evidential support" (Stanford Encyclopedia of Philosophy).

In his journal article "Faith as Doxastic Venture" found in "Religious Studies" by Cambridge University, John Bishop shares, "The doxastic venture model may thus be regarded as capturing the spiritual challenge of faith more satisfactorily than do models that conform to evidentialism. This is because, on the doxastic venture model, faith involves a deeper surrender of self-reliant control, not only in trusting God, but in accepting at the level of practical commitment that there is a God—indeed, *this* God—who is to be trusted."

Faith as Sub- or Non-Doxastic Venture

The term 'doxastic' is derived from the Greek word 'doxa,' which means 'belief' or 'opinion.' In philosophy, a doxastic venture is essentially a belief-based venture, where one's convictions and beliefs play a central role. On the other hand, a non-doxastic venture refers to a venture or aspect of life that does not rely on traditional beliefs or convictions.

Carl-Johan Palmqvist's work, "Desiderata for Rational, Non-Doxastic Faith," explores the concept of faith that does not depend on beliefs in the traditional sense. In this context, faith may be seen as something beyond the scope of conventional religious or ideological beliefs. Instead, it might involve trust, commitment, or engagement with something greater or transcendent that doesn't rely on doctrinal or belief-based foundations.

In a non-doxastic approach to faith, individuals engage in trust and commitment without the necessity of adhering to a set of religious or philosophical beliefs that align with traditional doctrines. This concept extends beyond the realm of religion and can be applied to various aspects of life, such as relationships, projects, or abstract principles. It underscores the idea that faith is not solely contingent on specific beliefs but can also thrive on trust and dedication.

Non-doxastic faith challenges the notion that faith is fundamentally tied to explicit beliefs. It suggests that faith can encompass a wider spectrum of human experiences, practices, and actions, all rooted in a deep sense of purpose or meaning. This perspective acknowledges that faith doesn't always neatly fit into traditional belief systems, allowing for a more diverse understanding of the concept.

Carl-Johan Palmqvist's work delves into the rationality of non-doxastic faith. This involves an exploration of whether it is possible to provide a coherent and rational justification or explanation for non-doxastic faith. It raises important questions about the compatibility of faith with reason and logic, shedding light on the intellectual underpinnings of this approach to faith.

Given that this work comes from the Department of Philosophy at Lund University, it also involves an interdisciplinary approach, drawing insights from philosophy, psychology, and theology to understand the nature of non-doxastic faith. This interdisciplinary lens allows for a more comprehensive understanding of the nature and implications of non-doxastic faith, enriching the discourse with diverse perspectives and methodologies.

Faith and Hope

At the core of human existence lies the profound and intertwined concepts of faith and hope. These two facets of the human experience often walk hand in hand, guiding us through the labyrinthine journey of life. While distinct in their essence, they share a deep connection, shaping our perspectives and attitudes towards the world around us.

Faith, in its essence, is the unwavering trust or confidence in something, be it a belief system, a person, or a cause. It serves as an anchor when the seas of uncertainty grow turbulent. Faith is often associated with religious or spiritual convictions, where individuals put their trust in a higher power or divine order. However, it can also manifest in various secular forms. One of the remarkable aspects of faith is its capacity to provide a sense of purpose and meaning, even in the absence of concrete evidence. It can be a guiding light through the darkest of times, offering solace and direction when the path ahead seems shrouded in obscurity. Faith allows individuals to take the leap into the unknown, driven by the conviction that something greater awaits on the other side.

Hope, on the other hand, is the beacon that illuminates the future, no matter how bleak the present may appear. It is the expectation or desire for something positive to occur, a belief that better days are ahead. Hope thrives on the belief that change is possible, and it fuels our determination to strive for a brighter tomorrow. Hope is not merely passive optimism; it's an active force that propels us to action. It motivates individuals to persevere through adversity, to pursue their dreams, and to work towards a better world. In times of despair, hope whispers that the sun will rise again, that healing and renewal are possible.

Faith and hope are not isolated entities; they often intersect and reinforce one another. Faith can nurture hope by providing a foundation of trust and confidence upon which hope can flourish. Likewise, hope can breathe life into faith, infusing it with the optimism needed to weather life's storms. Together, faith and hope offer a resilient response to life's uncertainties. They encourage us to face the unknown with courage and resilience, to believe in the possibility of transformation, and to find purpose even in the most challenging circumstances. Whether in the realm of spirituality, relationships, or personal growth, faith and hope are powerful allies in our journey through life's ever-unfolding narrative.

Faith as a Virtue

This idea of faith was considered and shared by Timothy Chappell. He wrote, "Faith is traditionally regarded as one of the 'theological' virtues. If a virtue is a 'disposition of character which instantiates or promotes responsiveness to one or more basic goods,' then theistic faith qualifies since it is 'a responsiveness to practical hope and truth,' provided theistic faith-claims are indeed true." Fiducial models of faith seem more attuned to exhibiting faith as a virtue, though a defense of the trustworthiness of the one who is trusted for salvation may be required.

Faith Beyond Orthodox Theism

When looking at faith not in relation to orthodox theism, one then leans in the direction of trust and belief. Generally, to believe in something, one must have knowledge of that thing. This form of belief is generally held by pragmatists. A few opinions were pulled from the Encyclopedia of Philosophy to show that there is a strong acceptance of the venture models of faith.

> The venture models, however, allow for the possibility that authentic faith may be variously realized, and be directed upon different, and mutually incompatible, intentional objects. This pluralism is an important feature of accounts of faith in the American pragmatist tradition. John Dewey strongly rejected the notion of faith as a special kind of knowledge (Dewey 1934, 20), as did William James, whose "justification of faith" rests on a *permissibility* thesis, under which varied and conflicting faith-commitments may equally have a place in the "intellectual republic" (James 1896 [1956, 30]). Charles S. Peirce, another influential American pragmatist, arguably held a non-doxastic view of faith.

> —Pope 2018

CHAPTER 7

The Correlation between Metaphysics and Faith

My main job is to awaken the knowledge and love for the divine things
that are already in your heart. You are a Soul. You are a child of God

— Harold Klemp

When looking for the correlation between metaphysics and faith, there are some real hardwired belief systems that make equitable analytical observatory findings difficult. What is sought here is not a concrete egocentric perspective filled with dogmatic naysayer results but an exploratory door opening review of selected past, present, and futuristic perspectives. This is very important as lifelong learning is essential to further this conversation beyond the borders of this text.

Philosophically, this very concept has Professor and Pro-Vice-Chancellor of Research of Manchester Metropolitan University, D. P. Gilroy, sharing the following:

The strategic significance of Lifelong Learning UK cannot be underestimated. It is the cornerstone of UK-wide policy to widen participation in education and training, to promote social inclusion and to increase prosperity. An increased participation in lifelong learning has the potential to enhance economic productivity and global competitiveness.

Why the grandiose explanation of the value of lifelong learning? It is my truth, but more importantly, it is the perfect segue into making the connection into the correlation between faith and metaphysics.

The noted founding figures of lifelong learning are Socrates, Plato, and Aristotle. These three philosophers believed and shared that one's intellect grows over time, so long as the mind is utilized to ponder new concepts as the opportunities present themselves. According to one article, it is stated that, "Plato and Aristotle added metaphysical arguments to support their systems of thought. Both outlined a specific sequence of studies to develop the powers of reasoning, and both established institutions wherein students and scholars could pursue learning for an indefinite period of time. Both Plato and Aristotle believed that certain sorts of study enabled the philosopher to engage in a lifetime of study that propelled toward his ideal" as pointed out by Rosa B. Lewis in her writing, "The Philosophical Roots of Lifelong Learning."

When looking at the correlation between metaphysics and faith, with the collective acceptance that the one semi-universal rationalization of faith would be a strong belief in something or someone with which there is no tangible evidence to provide proof to support the level of belief, and that metaphysics is the branch of philosophy that deals with the first principles of things, including abstract concepts such as being, knowing, substance, cause, identity, time, and space, the two terms do have a few relational ties.

The correlation between metaphysics and faith is a longstanding and endearing one. From a theological perspective, although this has not been substantiated or proven but does stand to reason, Eve in fact had some metaphysical ponderings. This thought is introduced for you to consider when Eve was approached in the garden; she was alone and pondering. The serpent as it is told assured her that if she did eat of the tree, she surely would not die but be as gods knowing good from evil. Eve then pondered that thought and responded.

> And when the woman saw that the tree was good for food,
> and that it was pleasant to the eyes, and a tree to be desired
> to make one wise, she took of the fruit thereof, and did eat,
> and gave also unto her husband with her; and he did eat.
>
> —Genesis 3:6 KJV

It was also at this pivotal point that Eve put her faith in what the serpent had shared with her as opposed to what God shared with Adam. Why? Could it have been that Satan addressed what was already a thought that Eve had in mind? Is it possible that Eve was the original founder of the "if-then" thought process? She made some clear, reasonable deductions. She was utilizing her senses. She saw that the tree was good for food, and it was also pleasant to the eyes. Additionally, it was wholistically a tree to be desired to make one wise, then based on the tangible data, she ate from the tree.

Then we have Adam knowing that God instructed him directly not to eat the fruit. He then put his faith in Eve as opposed to God and did eat the fruit. This has always been an area of concern for me. Some say that Eve tricked Adam. I wonder, did Adam apply the same rational reasoning that Eve did to the situation? In Genesis 2, God said:

> *And the Lord God commanded the man, saying,*
> *Of every tree of the garden thou mayest freely eat:*
> *But of the tree of the knowledge of good and evil, thou shalt not*
> *eat of it: for in the day that thou eatest thereof thou shalt surely die.*
>
> *—Genesis 2:16-17*

Well, Adam saw that Eve had eaten from the tree, and she was still alive. So, it stands to reason that if Adam ate from the tree, he would also live. Lo and behold, according to Scripture, Adam did live.

So, was his deductive reasoning wrong? That is a question for another time. What we learn from Scripture, which is considered by many as a priori knowledge, is that God was not pleased with the decision of Adam to eat with Eve, again over following what God told him. Genesis 3:17 (KJV) reads,

> *And unto Adam he said, Because thou hast hearkened unto the voice of thy wife, and hast eaten of the tree, of which I commanded thee, saying, Thou shalt not eat of it.*

This all comes together in Genesis 3:20 (KJV), which reads,

> *And Adam called his wife's name Eve; because she was the mother of all living.*

When we look to identify a definition for the name *Eve* or the term *Eve*, what is provided in the online dictionary is "the day or period of time immediately before an event or occasion" or "the beginning of something new." Her name alone has metaphysical implications. This information was shared as an attempt to show that the correlation between metaphysics and faith begins with the wondering why certain beliefs are what they are, where did they originate from, and is that perceived originating place really the originating concept, and is that originating concept satisfiable?

Again, according to Stewart W. Mirsky's article "Faith Metaphysics and Belief," he conjectures that in fact, there are really two types of faith, one being 'religious faith' and the other "tentative faith." Mr. Mirsky suggests that over all the faith that is placed in areas other than religion is tentative. This according to the author is described as the 'faith' one places in government. This faith is a very strong belief in a system that is unfounded and oftentimes cannot be explained, but generally exists because of what has been passed down through generations or via hearsay. However, with this tentative faith, additional reasoning and/or a perceived unkempt promise, faith in that system can be withdrawn. Mr. Mirsky goes even further to explain that in fact, that was not "faith" but a "strong" ordinary belief. He then goes on to share what he believes religious faith to be.

Religious faith is not tentative, as is said by Mr. Mirsky. Religious faith consists of "belief in some claim despite lack of evidence or proof for it." He goes on to share that "no amount of alternative information can normally shake us from our beliefs. If a prophet appeared tomorrow to deny what a prior prophet, in whom we had placed our faith today, had said, we would be moved to reject him or her because of the denial." The takeaway here is that according to Mr. Mirsky, if one can be turned away from their beliefs, then they are possibly not exercising "religious faith but tentative faith."

In accordance with this view and with what happens to so many who attempt to make blanket statements and conjectures, this is not an accurate representation of all those facts or his fact. As a close reading within the same writing, Mr. Mirsky states, "This is not to say that we could not be swayed. A sufficiently powerful personality or, perhaps, some overpowering events (the new prophet's capacity to produce miracles) could always entice us to switch allegiance, of course." One would indicate that as allegiances change, then the faith should also change; however, according to Mr. Mirsky, again he says, "But, in the end, it is allegiance that is at issue here, not differing facts. Religious faith is like saluting, giving our loyalty to one flag rather than another." He does acknowledge that generally, religious faith is not based on empirical data, so therefore, it cannot readily be measured the same as ordinary or tentative faith.

Another area that was available for review came from TruthUnity. Net. This site appears to be grappling with the concept of metaphysics and faith. On their homepage under the name is a subheading that reads, "A Fillmore Fellowship of Metaphysical Christians." Again, this is not to promote this group or any group's ideologies, but it is interesting to review what they are sharing as this research is concerning metaphysical manipulation of one's faith. What I can share about this group will be taken directly from their website to ensure an accurate representation.

To begin, the title of the writing is "Metaphysical, Meaning of Faith (RW)." There is no explanation for the "RW," so its definition is unknown. There is a prescribed definition of faith, and it is found below.

> *Faith—The perceiving power of the mind linked with the power to shape substance. Spiritual assurance; the power to do the seemingly impossible. It is a magnetic power that draws unto us our heart's desire from the invisible spiritual substance. Faith is a deep inner knowing that that which is sought is already ours for the taking. "Now faith is assurance of things hoped for"*
>
> —Hebrews 11:1

There is also an assortment of materials for Metaphysical Bible Study, including a "Metaphysical Bible Dictionary," a "Fenton Bible," a "Metaphysical Bible Study Guide," and a host of books and writings by several different authors. A few of the repeated authors are Mark Hicks, Ed Rabel, Charles Fillmore, Eric Butterworth, and Elizabeth S. Turner in addition to resources from the Unity School. They have recently transcribed "Unity Bible Lessons" that originated between 1895 and 1965. The web page explains that these are lessons that did not make it into the "Metaphysical Bible Dictionary."

Nevertheless, there is a "Fillmore Study Bible" called "World English Bible, Metaphysically Interpreted." There are both Old and New Testament interpretations. There is a Unity School of Practical Christianity.

What I found most interesting is that metaphysical Christians align themselves with evangelical Christians and say that they are just two opposite ends of the spectrum. Here is a quote from a member of the Unity Metaphysical Christian Community, named Mark: "Metaphysical Christianity and Evangelical Christianity are two ends of a continuum in Christian history and theology. One is focused on the person of Jesus and the adoration of his divinity, the other is focused on the Christ within, and the calling, in the words of Jesus, to love as he loved and to do the works that he did….How do we proclaim ourselves part of the historic Christian church without associating our theology with blood-atonement orthodox theology?"

It appears that the correlation between metaphysics and faith as it relates to this Christian group is one of putting one's faith into action.

CHAPTER 8

Are Metaphysics, Faith, and Religion Connected?

"Realize that everything connects to everything else."

—Leonardo da Vinci

I nitially, when looking into metaphysical manipulation of one's faith, I believe that this disease called tunnel vision began to overtake the "philosophical study" that was being conducted. With that, the original focus was on church leaders trying to take advantage of people to get rich and move on. Thankfully, what this research has led me to understand is that in some instances, my founding thoughts were validated; however, overwhelmingly, what research shows is that many of the faith-based systems were not established to "manipulate people's faith" but to enlighten people to a newly found way of considering "the beginning and how or who established everything," and the best ways to show appreciation for the gift given and ways to help others show their appreciation in addition to living up to what is perceived to be the creators prescribed way of life.

This is where organized religion comes in for consideration. To look at how metaphysics, faith, and religion are connected, we need to identify what constitutes a religion. Not too long ago, I did a study in which a brief look was taken at some established belief systems that were termed "religions," but a few authors referred to those belief systems as cults.

With that, let's establish a foundational definition for the term *religion* so there is no question or wavering about what is being discussed within this text. According to the Oxford Dictionaries, *religion* is defined as "the belief in and worship of a superhuman power or powers, especially a God or gods."

This research has led to several historic correlations as well as some modern-day influences. We will examine a few. One modern-day philosopher, William Lane Craig, fit in with a new way of considering the beginning of the world. Mr. Craig's basis for his metaphysical theories comes from a cosmological perspective with its sub-basis in Islamic belief systems.

Craig is a studied theologian with a PhD in philosophy. In addition, Craig has a doctorate in theology and is a well-known published author. In fact, Craig is most known for his contributions to the metaphysical and theological discussion of the existence of God. Craig coined the phrase "the kalam cosmological argument." In a writing entitled *Reasonable Faith*, Craig expressed that he was drawn to further purse this photophysical discourse because Al-Ghazali, who is described as one of the greatest medieval protagonists, had a very strong opinion of how Muslim philosophers were being influenced to deny God's creation of the universe by Greek philosophy.

Al-Ghazali was a Persian Muslim theologian. He began his discourse with a very sharp critique of the views of the day. This text was entitled *The Incoherence of the Philosophers*. Without moving too far from the discussion of the connectedness of metaphysics, faith, and religion, Al-Ghazali's basic argument is "the idea of a beginningless universe is absurd. The universe must have a beginning, since nothing began to exist without a cause, there must be a transcendent Creator of the universe."

This shows the metaphysical influential impact of his positioning as shared by Craig. Now to share Craig's perspectives, we will look to another philosopher.

Craig's perspectives have been very simply put into three components as they were shared by Curtis J. Metcalfe in his thesis submitted to the Graduate School at the University of Missouri-St. Louis. The thesis is titled "Defense of the Kalam Cosmological Argument and the B-Theory of Time."

Though Mr. Metcalfe agrees with the basis of the Kalam cosmological philosophical perspective, he does disagree with the A-theory of time, which is possibly the foundational pillar of the Kalam cosmological argument in favor of the B-theory of time. According to Mr. Metcalfe, William Lane Craig's views are as follows:

1. Whatever begins to exist has a cause of its *existence*.
2. The universe began to exist.
3. Therefore, the universe has a cause of its *existence*.

To be transparent, it is important to have a foundational understanding of both A-theory and B-theory of time. When considering the theories about time, both A and B have strengths and weaknesses as with everything in philosophy. It is simply a comparison between 'present' and 'eternity.' A-theory of time holds the perspective that things are happening in the moment, and there is no past or future for what is happening now in the present. B-theory of time holds that past, present, and future are equally real and responsible for each other.

One of the strongest proponents of the B-theory who has had a prolific impact on Mr. Metcalfe is John McTaggart.

Mr. McTaggart is given an honorable mention at this time due to his academic, political, and religious belief systems, and more importantly because he was an English idealistic metaphysician. He was most notably known for his writings and lectures around the concept that "time is unreal." In addition to his 1908 writing of "The Unreality of Time," he was an atheist, believed in human immortality, was a strong voice for the women's suffrage movement, was a defender of the Church of England, and was one of Bertrand Russell's adversaries. So much so that it was McTaggart's influence that led to the expulsion of Bertrand Russell from Trinity. This is a clear indication of the relationship between metaphysics, faith, and religion.

Jaegwon Kim, a Korean American philosopher, also speaks to this very closely linked relationship between metaphysics, faith, and religion. We are considering Dr. Kim's works because he conducted a great deal of his research on the philosophy of the mind. The reason this particular philosopher is the topic of study is because of his rejection of Cartesian metaphysics and his acceptance of dualism of another sort. Kim suggests "that while some mental states (intentional mental states, such as beliefs and desires) can be reduced to physical sources in the brain, other mental states, (phenomenal mental states, such as sensations) cannot be reduced to physical sources and are epiphenomenal."

What this shows is that there is indeed a strong interconnectedness between metaphysics, faith, and religion. This intertwining of the three is so entangled that the very notion of looking to one without addressing any of the others is basically impossible. As shared earlier, if one identifies as an atheist, they still share an alignment to an organized belief system requiring faith to establish and maintain an underlying belief of how everything began.

CHAPTER 9

How Does the Relationship between Metaphysics and Faith Impact Religion?

God is an hypothesis, and, as such, stands in need of proof:
the onus probandi (burden of proof) rests on the theist.

—Percy Bysshe Shelley

The relationship between metaphysics and faith and its impact on religion is a long-standing and endearing one. Earlier, we reviewed the interconnectedness of metaphysics, faith, and religion. It was shared that the metaphysical wondering of individuals led to believed answers to the following questions: "How did the world come into existence, and who created it?" As the believed answer appears plausible, individuals put their faith in the creation story, and due to that shared belief system, a new cultural system is established repeatedly. This new cultural system focuses on pleasing who or what is believed to have created the world as to stay in those initiates "good graces"; hence, there is the formulation of religion.

When looking to ascribe a definitive definition to the term religion, it was ever changing according to which and whose perspective the term was being defined. Oxford Dictionaries defines 'religion' as the belief in and worship of a superhuman controlling power, especially a personal god or gods. If one was to view the Collins English Dictionary, 'religion' is belief in a god or gods and the activities that are connected with this belief, such as praying or worshiping in a building such as a church or temple. A further consultation with ScienceDaily to define or understand the term 'religion' led to "Religion is an organized collection of beliefs, cultural systems, and world views that relate humanity to an order of existence. Many religions have narratives, symbols, and sacred histories that are intended to explain the meaning of life and/or to explain the origin of life or the Universe."

However, as we have become more global in our perspectives and worldviews, we need to be mindful not to define religion according to one's cultural norm and bias as to do so would eliminate the thoughts and experiences of so many others and would ultimately render this text and its finding useless as the basis of my findings would be biased. There is a newer more global explanation or definition of religion that appears to be inclusive, and it is what scholars are calling a functional definition of religion. One well-known example of this kind of definition refers to religion as "a system of beliefs and practices by means of which a group of people struggles with the ultimate problems of human life" (Yinger 1970, 7).

As with every potential term that may cause confusion, whenever the term 'religion' is utilized within this text, it is being utilized with the collective understanding that religion is the term being utilized to mean "a system of beliefs and practices by means of which a group of people struggles with the ultimate problems of human life."

With this understanding of religion, Plato's Euthyphro dilemma still stands. The question is posed by Socrates: "Is the pious loved by the gods because it is pious, or is it pious because it is loved by the gods?" This is shared as a lingering thought while reviewing how the relationship between metaphysics and faith impacts religion.

Researching different sources to truthfully identify the impact that metaphysics and faith has on religion led me to a religious group identified as TruthUnity. What is interesting about this group is their self-identification as "metaphysical Christians." A further review of their website revealed that this religion associates itself within the category of New Thought Christians and identifies as a movement. There were other branches that were not sustained for whatever reason; however, this one branch in particular has been able to withstand time.

According to Mark Hicks, the founder of TruthUnity and the author of the text shared on the TruthUnity website, the sustainability of this branch is directly correlated to the teachings of Charles Fillmore. Charles Fillmore followed and taught what he termed the Jesus Christ standard. According to the website of TruthUnity, the Jesus Christ standard is to focus on the Christ within. It appears that according to Charles Fillmore, the only way to practice the Jesus Christ standard, a follower must do everything according to how Jesus did it. They must be "focused on the Christ within, and the calling, in the words of Jesus, to loves as he loved and to do the works that he did."

Mark Hicks was sure to segregate metaphysical Christianity from evangelical Christianity by indicating that evangelical Christians focus more on the adoration of Christ and his works while metaphysical Christians lived to replicate the works of Christ. Hicks also provided some unsubstantiated data when he shared, "The 50%–75% of Americans who have dropped out of church are not dropping out of Christianity. They are just looking for a better story and a better way to practice their Christian faith."

It was not until a thorough review of many of the documents and resources provided by Mark Hicks that it became clear as to why this Christian religious group referred to themselves as metaphysical Christians. It is a part of the unsubstantiated data shared on the website: "They are just looking for a better story." They were revisiting the first principles of the Christian story to establish "a better story and a better way to practice their Christian faith."

TruthUnity is not in agreement with the concept of blood atonement; they see God as a principle not necessarily as a "god" in the sense of a person or persons. In addition, they believe that the Bible is not the only text that they need to live by in order to connect with the God inside of them.

As this text is not a review of the TruthUnity religion, there is no further need to share more of the very interesting and intriguing philosophical and theological premises. It must be clearly stated that the sharing of this information is in no way a check or seal of approval (as if I possessed that level of authority) of this belief system. One additional component of information that can inform this study pool of information was how the founder of TruthUnity aligned it to Mary Baker Eddy's Christian Science.

The reference to Mary Baker Eddy's Christian Science as a metaphysical Christian religion needs further review as this relates to how metaphysics and faith impact religion. Mary Baker Eddy lived from 1821 to 1910. Eddy was a sickly child and suffered with a chronic illness for her entire life. It appears that in seeking healing for herself, she took refuge in the Bible to understand what was happening to her both physically and mentally. She also went to a Dr. Quimby, who it is believed, via the use of the science of health or mesmerism, healed her both mentally and physically. With this, she developed the Christian Science religion in which healings took place because of one's faith in God and the healing powers of the scriptures.

Mary Baker Eddy's Christian Science shared the belief that the healings that took place in the Bible could indeed take place during her time and now. Eddy founded what was called the Christian Science Movement and opened the Massachusetts Metaphysical College in 1879. One of her beginning and profound texts was published in 1872, which is called "Science and Health with Key to Scriptures." Her teachings embraced the Christian faith-based system from a whole other perspective—the scientific standpoint. Eddy's metaphysical perspective is that there is a scientific and spiritual correlation between one's physical and mental health. It was the teachings of the Metaphysical College that people who were ill both mentally and physically could be healed by their faith.

Again, one must remember that Mary Baker Eddy was a woman with some very radical perspectives during a male-dominated time. It is fair to speculate that many thoughts and perspectives that are shared in countless articles and writing about Mary Baker Eddy have some biases. Nevertheless, this is not an endorsement of her perspectives, only a very brief look at how metaphysics and faith impact religion.

My final thoughts of how metaphysics and faith impact religion are simply that they are profound. Reason being metaphysics is the study or philosophy of beginnings, faith is a deep belief in something even if there is not tangible evidence to support that level of trust, and religion is the practice of devotion born out of that faith in what is determined to have begun or established the world.

How is religion impacted by metaphysics and faith? The religious practices of a group will be determined and established according to what that group believes the beginnings to be. If the beginnings are believed to have been begun by a god, then they will revere that god. If by multiple gods, then there will be a reverence of the multitude of gods, and if the belief is that the beginning came from a big bang, then the beliefs and practices will be to cultivate an admiration of what caused the big bang. For all intents and purposes, religion is born from one's faith in their metaphysical understandings.

CHAPTER 10

What is Manipulation?

*Just because something isn't a lie does not mean that it isn't deceptive.
A liar knows that he is a liar, but one who speaks mere portions
of truth in order to deceive is a craftsman of destruction.*

—Criss Jami

Manipulation of people has been seen as a way to keep the enslaved, enslaved. Consider this: why would one need to shackle anyone's body when they can place a stronghold on their minds? Is it not the mind of man that controls their actions? This has been an area of discussion among many in differing segments of the religious, nonreligious, and scientific communities. What is it about manipulation that causes people such areas of great debates? Is manipulation bad? What constitutes manipulation? Are there other names for manipulation? Is there a relationship between manipulation and faith-based systems?

An attempt to answer these questions will take place in this portion of text. The supposed answers, more like responses, will come from the "experts" in the field of study concerning manipulation. To be clear, my analysis of the experts will take place in a later chapter of this book.

What is manipulation? After reviewing multiple texts, articles, and websites, it is my decision to utilize both the "Stanford Encyclopedia of Philosophy" to look at and review manipulation and, more importantly, the ethics of manipulation in addition to WebMD, "manipulation and the symptoms to look out for." Both sources will be referenced collaboratively as well as independently.

A refined definition of 'manipulation' came from shifting to the root word manipulate, which the Oxford online dictionary defines in two manners:

1. handle or control (a tool, mechanism, etc.), typically in a skillful manner
2. control or influence (a person or situation) cleverly, unfairly, or unscrupulously

It is my choice to share both methods as we consider the manipulation of texts (i.e., the Bible) in addition to other faith-based texts and people, their thoughts, feelings, emotions, and actions.

WebMD defines 'manipulation' in this manner: "Manipulation is the exercise of harmful influence over others. People who manipulate others *attack their mental and emotional sides* to get what they want." Wikipedia states that "*manipulation* in psychology is a *behavior designed to exploit, control, or otherwise influence* others to one's advantage." Identifying manipulation as a "behavior" is further defined as "the range of actions and mannerisms made by individuals."

According to psychology Author George K. Simon, successful psychological manipulation primarily involves the manipulator:

- Concealing aggressive intentions and behaviors in addition to being affable
- Knowing the psychological vulnerabilities of the victim to determine which tactics are likely to be the most effective
- Having a sufficient level of ruthlessness to have no qualms about causing harm to the victim if necessary

Dr. G. K. Simon sums up his statement with these words: "Consequently, the manipulation is likely to be covert; relational aggressive or passive-aggressive." Although the language seems to appear somewhat harsh, it is in alignment with almost all the research that has been conducted. Actually, according to "Stanford Encyclopedia of Philosophy," prior to an action being identified as manipulative, there are two questions that should be deliberated over. The questions are, can the actions or behaviors be defined/identified and evaluated? This is essential to the utilization of the term 'manipulation' as every form of influence, which is defined as "the capacity to have an effect on the character, development, or behavior of someone or something, or the effect itself" (Oxford Dictionary of World Languages), is not manipulative. However, it is important to retain the notion that both identification and evaluation are supportive of one another to the determination of manipulation.

When looking to identify the behavior or the behaviors to determine the classification of manipulation, what must be objectively contemplated is what in fact were the behaviors. According to the research shared in the "Stanford Encyclopedia of Psychology," there are three characteristics of manipulation. They are as follows:

1. Influence that does not consider rational deliberation
2. Influence when pressure is applied
3. Influence when trickery is utilized

All three of these areas will be reviewed to identify if these behaviors or actions could possibly be executed by faith-based leaders.

When considering the first characteristic, not only does the influencer not rationalize what they are sharing, but they do not allow for the one being manipulated to apply any reason to the situation. Actually, when this characteristic was further analyzed, what was taken away is that it is not entirely accurate. What does occur in most if not all situations is that when the target begins to think through the manipulator's desire, if they begin to question, that is when irrational considerations are applied. This is an alternate way of sharing that the target's reasonings are then further influenced to no end, except the manipulator's desired outcome.

According to research conducted by Joseph Raz, an Israeli philosopher, the manipulator introduces nonrational influences. Here is a thought: manipulation, unlike coercion, does not interfere with a person's options. Instead, it perverts the way that person reaches decisions, forms preference, or adopts goals (Raz 1988, 377).

The second characterization of manipulation is influence that includes pressure. When grappling with this form of manipulation, what is evident is that the types of pressure applied have a range. When considering the forms of pressure, there could be emotional blackmail and peer pressure. What is also key to this form of manipulation is that the target is not convinced but agrees anyway.

One example of this form of manipulation comes from a study conducted by Ruth R. Faden, Tom L. Beauchamp, and Nancy M. P. King in 1986 concerning a doctor-patient relationship. One finding was although the patient was not convinced, it is nonetheless awkward and difficult to resist this rather "controlling" physician (Faden, Beauchamp, and King 1986, 258).

When considering the third characteristic of manipulative influence, trickery, it is clearly along the lines of deception. This is because when looking for the definition of both terms, they share the same traits. Deception includes presenting a false reality, manipulating the fact, oftentimes lying. Trickery is also defined as causing people to believe a false reality, convincing someone that they are in possession of something or that they can achieve something that they cannot by presenting a false reality. Generally, the advertising industry is known for these types of tactics.

However, when considering the manipulative influence of trickery and deception from a more personal perspective, that is when both mental and physical harm can occur. If one were to consider Michael

Cholbi's observation that the phenomenon of ego depletion might induce targets of manipulation to form faulty intentions (that is, intentions that do not reflect their considered values) because their resistance to temptation has been worn down (Cholbi 2014).

A final consideration of influential manipulation in the form of trickery or deception is shared by Claudia Mills, a philosophy professor. Mills offers a theory that can be considered as either a version of or a close relative to the trickery account:

> *We might say, then, that manipulation in some way purports to be offering good reasons, when in fact it does not. A manipulator tries to change another's beliefs and desires by offering her bad reasons, disguised as good, or faulty arguments, disguised as sound—where the manipulator himself knows these to be bad reasons and faulty arguments* (see Benn 1967 and Gorin 2014b for somewhat similar ideas).

Considering these three characteristics of manipulation led to the review of multiple research studies and opinions. One consistent ideology was ever present, and that was the manipulator will do and say whatever is needed to reach the ultimate goal. Now with that, if the influencer is not willing to go to the extreme of creating a false reality, pressuring one to change their minds or to just do what they are telling them to do, perhaps manipulation is not the appropriate classification for what has or had occurred. According to the information, any two of the characteristics can be in operation at the same time, and there will be those instances where there will be an intertwining of all three characteristics. One researcher in particular, Joel Rudinow, makes the following claim: the use of pressure is manipulative only if the would-be manipulator directs it at some supposed weakness in his target that will render the target unable to resist it; this leads him to finalize his definition in terms of "deception or by playing upon a supposed weakness" of the target with the second disjunction meant to cover pressure-based tactics (Rudinow 1978, 346).

For these very reasons, it is essential that the second question concerning manipulation is always considered. That is the question of evaluation of the results and/or the intended results of the manipulator and the action of manipulation.

When evaluating a situation to determine the plausibility of manipulation, one is seeking to weigh the level of harm intended or implemented by the manipulative party. In this section, an overview of evaluating situations to check for manipulation will occur. There are philosophical and legal terms utilized when evaluating manipulation. Is it absolutely immoral, *pro tanto* immoral, *prima facie* immoral, etc.? It should also tell us *when* manipulation is immoral if it is not always immoral. Finally, a satisfactory answer to the evaluation question should tell us *why* it is immoral in cases when it is immoral.

It should be made very clear at this point that when considering the morality of manipulation, the opinions are as vast as there are stars in the sky. When utilizing terms like 'always,' 'absolute,' 'moral,' and 'immoral,' background information is essential to establish a plausible response. With that, and for the purposes of this writing, it must be stated that there is no absolute or always shared viewpoint. Move forward understanding that the if-then argument is always present.

How are evaluations conducted to judge manipulatory motives? To begin, as it is considered in research, the moral values associated with actions fall into three categories: pro tanto, prima facie, or moral particularism. The three terms are best explained as follows:

- pro tanto - to be wrong all the time unless it can be proven to be right
- prima facie - absolutely wrong
- moral particularism - the understanding that morality should not be determined according to principles but the consideration of the data related to the situation

As previously shared, when considering absolutism, there will always be areas for a loophole. One researcher, Allen Wood, suggested that the "moral" factor be removed when considering acts of manipulation. He shared this thought: if we think that moral argument should proceed not merely by invoking our pro- or con-sentiments or appealing to our unargued intuitions, but instead by identifying objective facts about a situation that give us good reasons for condemning or approving certain things, then we would generally do much better to use a nonmoralized sense of words like *coercion*, *manipulation*, and *exploitation*—a sense in which these words can be used to refer to such objective facts (Wood 2014, 19–20).

A less extreme position would be that while manipulation is always *pro tanto* wrong, other moral considerations can sometimes outweigh the *pro tanto* wrongness of manipulation.

—Stanford Encyclopedia of Philosophy

With the knowledge of what manipulation is or can be, one must question, is everyone manipulative? This is an essential question as the foundational question is looking to identify if metaphysical manipulation in faith-based systems is influencing people's faith.

In one particular research article shared by Sarah Regan, a spirituality and relationships writer, it looked at the very same question. This article was granted an expert review by Chamin Ajjan, LCSW, A-CBT, CST. In this article, ideas like projective identification, passive-aggressive behaviors, and so many other ways that manipulation occurs are discussed. What is shared is that all people are in fact manipulative at one point or another. The question is whether the levels of manipulation in everyone rise to the level of others, becoming absolutely convinced that what they think or feel has no value as it relates to that of the manipulation taking place. In other words, not all manipulation that occurs leads to a total shift in an individual's ideological perspective.

This article did share thirteen types of manipulative behaviors, which are the following: gaslighting, passive aggression, verbal abuse, lying, withholding affection or sex, love-bombing, praising, complaining, guilt-tripping, passive-aggressive posting online, projective identification, feigning innocence, and blaming. A brief explanation of each type of manipulation is necessary to ensure that a holistic review of metaphysical manipulation by faith-based leadership is done. This will take place in the next section.

CHAPTER 11

The Thirteen Types of Manipulation

There are those whose primary ability is to spin wheels of
manipulation. It is their second skin and without these
spinning wheels, they simply do not know how to function.
They are like toys on wheels of manipulation and control.

If you remove one of the wheels, they'll never
be able to feel secure, be whole.

—C. JoyBell C.

As was shared, there are currently thirteen types of manipulative behaviors to consider. Additional research did shed light on 'cruel humor' as a form of manipulation, which will also be briefly reviewed. It is not the intent to suggest that other forms of persuasion cannot or do not rise to the level of manipulation, but within this context, a review will only be conducted of the thirteen mentioned in the previous chapter.

Cruel Humor

According to WebMD, cruel humor was utilized as a form of manipulation. In a way to establish a sense of psychological superiority, it was shared that cruel humor is used by manipulators to jab at an individual's weaknesses to instill a feeling of insecurity. The more this is done, the more insecure the individual becomes. This is done both publicly and privately to make a person look bad.

Gaslighting

In the expert review of an article by Kristina Hallett, PhD, ABPP, gaslighting is a form of psychological manipulation that involves making someone question their own reality, feelings, and experiences of events in order to maintain control over that person. It is further shared that "gaslighting at its core is always about self-preservation and the maintenance of power/control—namely, the power/control to construct a narrative that keeps the gaslighter in the 'right' and their partner in the 'wrong,'" therapist Aki Rosenberg, LMFT, shared.

Passive Aggression

According to Dr. Daniel K. Hall-Flavin, who is board certified in General Psychiatry and Addiction Psychiatry, "Passive-aggressive behavior is a pattern of indirectly expressing negative feelings instead of openly addressing them."

To define this behavior clearer, there was a review of multiple texts and websites, but unfortunately, a clear definition of the two terms was unavailable. What was available was this explanation from Study.com: "A concise definition is difficult because the term 'passive-aggressive behavior' encompasses a number of actions and inactions. A good place to start is a trusted source of clarification, the Merriam-Webster's Dictionary, which defines passive aggressive as 'being, marked by, or displaying behavior characterized by the expression of negative feelings, resentment, and aggression in an unassertive *passive* way."

Dr. Preston Ni, MSBA, also shares that "passive-aggressiveness can be defined as anger or hostility in disguise, expressed in underhanded ways to exercise power, control, and deception, with the hopes of getting away with it."

Verbal Abuse

According to an article in WebMD that was medically reviewed by Dan Brennan, MD, "Verbal abuse, also known as emotional abuse, is a range of words or behaviors used to manipulate, intimidate, and maintain power and control over someone." The article goes on to share that "a part of the verbal abuse includes insults, humiliation, ridicule, the silent treatment, and attempts to scare, isolate, and control."

In an article published on Psych Central, a website that was medically reviewed by N. Simay Gökbayrak, PhD, in addition to the Scientific Advisory Board, additional insights were shared concerning verbal abuse. In this article entitled "How to Deal with Verbal Abuse," it is shared that there is a spectrum of verbal abuse. "Yelling and verbal abuse don't always go hand-in-hand. Verbal abuse can also be quiet, insidious, and subtle."

Withholding Affection

Initially, this topic may appear to be unrelated based on the topic of research; however, there may be a direct correlation to the withholding of affection as a form of manipulation within faith-based systems. According to Dr. George Simon, the withholding of affection is a form of manipulation that occurs randomly and deliberately without reason, other than to suit the need of the manipulator. The withholding of affection may be offset by 'intermittent reinforcements.' These reinforcements are a way to cause the person who is being manipulated not to see the manipulation, but to excuse it.

Love-Bombing

This term was explained by Wikipedia as "an attempt to influence a person by demonstrations of attention and affection." It can be used in different ways and for either positive or negative purposes. Psychologists have identified love-bombing as a possible part of a cycle of abuse and have warned against it. It has also been described as psychological manipulation in order to create a feeling of unity within a group against a society perceived as hostile.

Praising

According to Dr. Leon F. Seltzer, who is best known for his professional guidebook, "Paradoxical Strategies in Psychotherapy," in his article "Evolution of the Self, Praise as Manipulation: 6 Reasons to Question Compliments," he expresses that "praises can have an ulterior motive other than to express genuine approval and joy." Dr. Seltzer shares that praise can constitute a kind of verbal bribery, offered primarily to serve the interest of the person offering it. Dr. Seltzer warns of disingenuous praise with invisible strings (or a price tag) attached to it because such praise comes at a cost.

Complaining

The manipulator utilizes complaints in a way to convince the one being manipulated that they have in some way caused a problem. The complaints are generally unfounded and general in nature. The complaints are utilized to get the other party to agree to what the manipulator wants.

Guilt-Tripping

Liza Gold, a social worker and Founder and Director of Gold Therapy NYC, explains, "A guilt trip is best defined as the intentional manipulation of another person's emotions to induce feelings of guilt." In the article medically reviewed by Dr. Karin Gepp, PsyD, entitled "Why the 'Guilt Trip' Comes Naturally (but Can Be Problematic)," it is also shared that "guilt-tripping is a natural form of passive-aggression that people result to when they don't have the skills or language to assertively communicate their needs or feelings." There are instances when guilt-tripping can be toxic. Guilting is included in the eleven behavioral signs of emotional abuse in others, also shared on the psych central website.

Passive-Aggressive Posting Online

Initially, when this was mentioned, there was very little validity associated with it. Now, however, with the rise in social media and its use to shift markets and thinking, it must be included in this research.

In one article, passive-aggressive posting online was referred to as "covert and deliberate, and means that someone who is experiencing anger has chosen to post something online, that to some people, seems innocent, but to the person it is aimed at, it has shared meaning. This can range from very obvious meaning, like in the music video I was targeted with, or something more vague to cause worry and doubt. The aim of passive aggressive posting is to get revenge without blame" (Jacqueline Ward).

Because passive-aggressive posting online is so new, there is not a lot of qualitative information concerning this topic. What was interesting was the information gathered from Trisha Prabhu. She is a twenty-one-year-old innovator, social entrepreneur, global advocate, and inventor of ReThink™, a patented technology and an effective way to detect and stop online hate. She is currently pursuing her undergraduate degree at Harvard University. She has an online blog, in which she was supporting an individual experiencing passive-aggressive posting online. She reminded them, "To be clear: passive-aggressive behavior online can be very damaging and is never okay."

Projective Identification

When researching projective identification, the term 'psychological seesaw' came up. In an article entitled "Projective Identification: The Psychological Seesaw" written by Lisa Schlesinger, a psychoanalyst and also an LCSW-C, it was explained that a person's individual internal reality can be swayed by the projection of another individual. According to Lisa Schlesinger, "It's almost as if the projector is weighed down by negative parts of the self, and they hand those parts off to another person, weighing down the receiver. It's like the mind is saying, "This doesn't belong to me. You hold it."

As projective identification relates to manipulation, it is seen as a way to project self-negative traits and attributes onto another individual and then accuse the individual of the negative attribute while the person receiving the negative attacks does not exhibit the trait initially, but begins to believe that they do. Projective identification was initially coined by and is a key feature of Klein's paranoid-schizoid position.

Feigning Innocence

According to Wikipedia, feigning innocence is when the manipulator tries to suggest that any harm done was unintentional or that they did not do something that they were accused of. The manipulator may put on a look of surprise or indignation. This tactic makes the victim question their own judgment and possibly their own sanity.

This explanation of feigning innocence is presented by Author Dr. George K. Simon. Dr. Simon writes that successful psychological manipulation primarily involves the manipulator. Dr. George K. Simon holds a PhD in psychology and is the author of "In Sheep's Clothing: Understanding and Dealing with Manipulative People," a 1996 book about psychological manipulation.

Blaming

According to dictionary.com, 'blaming' is defined as "to hold responsibility; find fault with; censure: to place the responsibility for (a fault, error, etc.) (usually followed by *on*)." Those were the definitions as verbs. But when looking at 'blaming' as a noun, the definitions are as follows: "an act of attributing fault; censure; reproof: responsibility for anything deserving of censure."

When considering blaming as a part of manipulation, George Simon, PhD, explains that by habitually blaming others for one's own indiscretions, the individual resists modifying the problematic attitudes and behavior patterns.

Another article referred to this as victim-blaming. According to this article on exploring your mind, victim-blaming manipulation consists of one person violating the other person psychologically so that they (the blamer) aren't questioned.

* * *

After reviewing all thirteen types of manipulation, there is room to see how each type can occur within a faith-based belief system, more specifically in Christianity. There are times when within Christianity, people can be gaslighted to believe that they are possessed by a demon. There are other instances when individuals may go to a house of worship seeking help, and they are given a series of things that they must do to receive salvation. What about when different ministries are formed and people are charged to participate, and if they do not, then they are ignored by the church leadership? A final connection is when individuals come into places of worship believing that they are dressed well, and cruel jokes are made addressing their attire. Again, if we pay attention, all thirteen forms of manipulation can be found in many houses of worship.

CHAPTER 12

Breach of Trust in Faith-Based Leadership (Religion)

The very essence of religion is to adjust the mind and soul of man.

—Charles Allen

C harles Allen was a nationally known Methodist minister, born in 1913, and laid to rest in 2005. Throughout his years as a minister, he wrote columns in local papers (Georgia and Texas), hosted both television and radio shows, pastored, and published books. One book in particular that sold over a million copies is "God's Psychiatry," first published in 1953. What is so compelling is the caption under the book's title. The caption reads, "With faith you can work miraculous changes in your life—in seven days."

This is intriguing. Can the preacher, pastor, author, television, and radio show host ensure that in seven days, by a person's faith, they will receive miraculous changes in their life? I am not sure. This also leads to the further wondering of why did this book in particular sell so many copies? Is it the integrity of the text or the influence of its author? Has this minister manipulated the level of trust that he had over the people and utilized it for financial gain? Again, I do not know. Did he perhaps give away the books? Again, that information is not available.

This may seem simple and looks as if a minister is encouraging people to have and exercise faith. Maybe it is harmless; nevertheless, in the next section, there will be a review of other faith-based systems to gain additional insight on mental manipulation within faith-based systems. For now the question is, has there been a breach in faith-based leadership? The question alone may come across as an indictment, but in fact, there are numerous instances of faith-based leaders caught doing wrong things. Let's consider the question but remove the scandalous connotations. In this section, the only area of concern is the manipulation of an individual's faith.

According to the different texts, websites, and scholarly journals, a breach of trust placed in faith-based leadership has been in existence from the beginning of faith-based leadership. Initially when considering this question, it was not as apparent as the research revealed.

The many different congregations, denominations, religious belief systems, and atheism all stem from a breach in faith-based leadership. With this, a better question to consider is why? Why have people placed so much trust in faith-based leaders? What is it that would cause a person to believe another person beyond reason and in some instances to the point of death? The one response that is glaring is spiritual manipulation.

Spiritual manipulation, according to June Hunt, a biblical counselor, as written in her book entitled "Manipulation: Cutting the Strings of Control," is the use of religious words or acts to manipulate someone for personal gain or to achieve a personal agenda, thereby harming that person's walk with God. She goes on to share that "at the core of spiritual manipulation is control of others. Spiritual manipulation is acting 'Spiritual' to benefit oneself by using self-centered efforts to control others."

With this definition and explanation, one can consider how many times leaders in faith-based systems have used their positions of spiritual authority to impress upon their followers to do things that were beneficial to them. Perhaps the selling of indulgences or telling people that God is going to give them a special blessing for the gift to the pastor or their spouse. How many times have people stood in prayer lines, only to be asked to give a special donation for the prayer? And the list goes on.

One Baptist minister, Howard Pittman, who experienced a near-death experience, believed that he was led to write a book dealing with the deceptive and complacent state of the 'church.' The text is titled "Placebo: What Is the Church's Dope?" What is most interesting is the cover of the book.

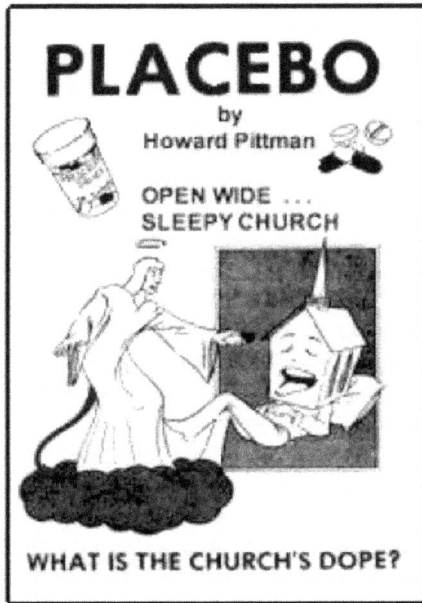

As you can see from the very vivid depiction of the church, it is laid back in an overly comfortable state, accepting all types of sedating medications prescribed by a deceptive image of Jesus. However, a closer look clearly shows that Satan has prescribed and is administering/ feeding the church the sedatives.

When looking at the cover and reading the text, its alignment with this topic became very apparent. Are church leaders pushing what Minister Pittman referred to as a sugar-coated religion? Throughout his writing, he makes several references to manipulative practices and the immediate impact that they have. In one section, he shares how church members go to church and participate in all types of church activities except for "practicing the type of life that they are professing with their mouths." They must always seek the opinion of the leader and not take the advice of any other leader. Generally, the prevailing sentiment around wrongdoing is "we all do it and just cannot help it."

He also shared how he was teaching and preaching and leading people to Christ. One would conjecture that this is good, but it wasn't, as all he was doing was for self-glorification and self-edification. It wasn't about the people or about the great commandment. Again, this is why it is essential to understand that manipulation is not always apparent, and the breach in faith-based leadership can go unnoticed. Minister Pittman acknowledged that he had become what he called "my own false god."

The information shared by Minister Pittman in his book has been and is still being read by individuals of different denominations and across many parts of the world. This shows a breach in the trust placed in faith-based leadership.

Looking back to June Hunt's text, she shared six pointed ways in which spiritual leaders manipulate others with their place of authority. They are as follows:

1. *The religious leader* who uses guilt to compel attendance, financial giving, or service
2. *The religious counselor* who takes emotional or sexual advantage of a counselee in the name of 'comfort' or 'compassion'
3. *The religious people* who accuse those who disagree with them of being rebellious against God
4. *The religious husband* who demands submission from his wife as a means of control, getting her to placate his selfishness

5. *The religious parent* who commands total, unquestioned compliance from children and uses harsh discipline without compassion or understanding

6. *The religious employer* who micromanages employees, expecting them to work long hours without equitable monetary compensation

In the above examples taken from the book "Manipulation: Cutting the Strings of Control," it shows that any religious person with authority over another person is deemed a religious leader.

When further considering if there has been a breach in the trust placed in faith-based leaders, in the "Stanford Encyclopedia of Philosophy," while reviewing the ethics of manipulation, the topic of manipulating persons versus manipulating situations was mentioned. Looking at the manipulation of situations can align with a breach in the trust placed in faith-based leadership. Consider the scenario described below:

> *Consider Joel Rudinow's example of a malingerer who manipulates a psychiatrist into admitting him to the psychiatric ward (Rudinow 1978). He does this by fooling a police officer into thinking he is about to commit suicide. The police officer brings him to the ward, reports that he is suicidal, and requests that he be admitted. Although the psychiatrist is not fooled, her hospital's rules force her to admit the malingerer at the police officer's request.*

In the above shared writing, we see both the manipulation of people and a situation. The police officer mentioned above was manipulated to believe that the individual would harm himself. Having an understanding of the law, he knew that if he could convince the police officer, the officer would have to take him to the hospital, and he would have to be admitted. The psychiatrist was not fooled, but due to situational manipulation, there was no other alternative.

With situational manipulation, the manipulator controls the situation and creates an unfair self-advantage that, in some cases, can cause harm to or distress to others, not only the intended target. An example of this could be when the faith-based leaders intentionally plan a revival within the first six days of the month and request an inflated monetary amount to ensure that everything goes well, knowing that a majority of the parishioners live on a monetary benefit that is issued within the first three days of the month.

Another example could be when the leaders call a meeting, and prior to ending the meeting, specific requests are made openly to individuals in the group, and because they do not want to appear negative, they stay and honor the request. However, by them staying, they have caused the person giving them a ride to stay as well. In this scenario, due to the manipulation of the situation, the driver was compelled to stay.

William Riker created a term for this type of manipulation—heresthetic. 'Heresthetic,' according to Riker, is simply "structuring the world so you can win" (1986). Riker's term heresthetic, is so relevant to this topic of mental manipulation, as many church leaders redesign, present, and/ or reimagine the Gospel Message of Christ to ensure that ultimately, they win. They win power over the people's thoughts, actions, and wallets. Again, I want to be transparent by sharing that not every proclaimer of the Gospel behaves in this manner. Unfortunately, they have and are causing damage to people as they take what they can from them.

Further down in the "Stanford Encyclopedia of Philosophy," Anne Barnhill's research is considered. Anne Barnhill distinguishes between manipulation that "changes the options available to the person or changes the situation she's in, and thereby changes her attitudes" on the one hand, and manipulation that "changes a person's attitudes directly without changing the options available to her or the surrounding situation" on the other (Barnhill 2014, 53).

When considering this form of manipulation within the faith-based system, it can be considered as sacrilege. According to this information, manipulation can be of people, situations, or items all gleaning adherence from deontological ethics.

CHAPTER 13

Faith-Based Systems/ Religions

The truth is more important than the facts.

—Frank Lloyd Wright

I t is essential to review actions taken by religious leaders to consider, "Has there been a breach in the trust placed in faith-based leadership?" The review will include a brief synopsis of a few faith-based systems. Although it may appear that this text is seeking to place an indictment against these systems, that is not the case. It is not my goal to misrepresent myself as an authority of any other faith than Christianity, so I am clearly stating that my reporting will include information from "Cults, World Religions, and the Occult by Kenneth Boa and The Story of the Christian Church" by Jesse Lyman Hurlbut, in addition to information shared publicly in libraries and other searchable areas.

The faith-based systems selected and the information presented does not reflect any personal allegiance or biases as there is a representation of both non-Christian and Christian. The systems reviewed are Christian religions, non-Christian religions of the east, pseudo-Christian religions of the west, and some additional religions.

Christian Religions

Roman Catholic Church

To begin, the Roman Catholic Church is believed to be the largest Christian church with a worldwide membership of over a billion believers. According to britannica.com, "Roman Catholicism can be traced to the life and teachings of Jesus Christ in Roman-occupied Jewish Palestine about 30 CE." Catholicism is a form of Christianity. It is said to be the original Christian faith-based belief system that has a direct connection to Jesus via the disciples. According to several different texts, Catholicism is responsible for sharing Christianity around the world. Within the Catholic faith, there are a few very defined beliefs, practices, and hierarchical positioning that one must adhere to. Additionally, the gender roles were clearly defined at one point.

Within the Catholic faith, there are seven sacraments that are followed: baptism, reconciliation (formerly known as penance), the Eucharist, matrimony, ordination, confirmation, and anointing of the sick. These sacraments are the cornerstones of the faith as well as a part of the plan to salvation. According to Catholicism, faith in Jesus Christ and grace is not enough for justification. One must also keep the seven sacraments.

In the Eucharist, when the Catholic believer eats the body and drinks the blood, the believer accepts the idea that the items are changed into the actual body and blood of Christ. This is called transubstantiation.

According to the online Encyclopedia Britannica, the hierarchy structure is as follows: "The pope appoints and presides over the cardinals, whose numbers grew dramatically in the late 20th century, reaching 182 under John Paul II (1978–2005). Each of the church's 500 archbishops is the head of an archdiocese. These in turn are divided into about 1,800 dioceses, each headed by a bishop. Within dioceses are parishes, each served by a church and a priest." These sacraments are important as in the Catholic faith-based system, the Church is equally authoritative as the Bible. By the "Church," this term is referring to the leaders, popes, archbishops, and bishops. Within the Catholic faith, they also follow baptism by submersion under water or by the pouring of water three times on the person's head.

Another area within the Catholic faith is the praying to the saints, confession to the heads of the church, and the idea that the pope is like a substitute for Christ and purgatory. These areas of belief are significant in the Catholic faith as purgatory represents a place between death and heaven. It is believed to be a place of final purification where the believer can go through a final process so they will be able to be presented before God.

Additionally, Catholic believers pray to the pope and Mary, the mother of Jesus, as intermediaries between them and God. This level of reverence goes along with the doctrine of Assumption, which, according to Wikipedia, has two explanations: "The Catholic Church has two different traditions concerning the assumption/dormition of Mary: in the first, she rose from the dead after a brief period and then ascended into heaven; in the second, she was "assumed" bodily into heaven before she died."

Protestantism

"Protestantism is the largest grouping of Christians in the United States, with its combined denominations collectively comprising about 43% of the country's population (or 141 million people) in 2019. Other estimates suggest that 48.5% of the U.S. population (or 157 million people) is Protestant" (Wikipedia 2019). This is not to confuse the statement concerning the Catholic Church about them being the largest worldwide. There are some distinct differences and some similarities. This review is not to create a comparative summation but to identify the differences between the two faith-based systems.

Protestantism was birthed out of the Protestant Reformation. It is believed by many that the Protestant faith-based system was initiated by Martin Luther. Martin Luther was a monk and a professor at the University of Gothenburg in Germany. What made the Reformation so impactful was that great Christian leaders around Europe began to share their concerns publicly. There was John Calvin, Huldrych Zwingli (a pastor), Frederick the Wise (a very influential political leader who was responsible for upholding the law as the elector of Saxony), Philip Melanchthon (a theologian), John Wycliffe (another theologian), John Knox, and many others.

These leaders believed in 'sola scriptura,' that the Bible is the sole authority for the life of the Christian. They were not in agreement with the Catholic Church's belief that Church leadership held the same authority as the Bible.

In general, one of the main premises of the Reformers/Protestants is that salvation in Christianity came by the faith in the blood atonement of Jesus Christ and nothing else. This is referred to as 'sola fide.' Additionally, according to the Protestant faith, no human is perfect, and the only perfect human was Jesus. With this, members of the Protestant faith pray in "Jesus's name" as the intercessor between God and man, which leads to the two sacraments of this faith-based system, which are the Lord's supper and baptism.

As was already shared, baptism is conducted by the full immersion of the believer in water.

When it comes to the Lord's supper, there is a divide among Protestant believers. Some believe that when taking (eating the bread and drinking the wine), the elements go through what is called consubstantiation. This means that Jesus is present during this time and is blessing the elements and those who are receiving them. Then there are others who believe that the Lord's supper is taken to commemorate the action of Jesus giving his body and shedding his blood as the ultimate sacrifice for man's redemption. For these believers, the elements are symbolic and do not go through any form of transformation.

The Protestant faith places a heavy emphasis on the indwelling of the Holy Spirit. This emphasis is placed as according to the Protestant faith, it is the Holy Spirit that leads, guides, and equips people to live the life that God wants by revealing God's message as shared by the Bible. Along those lines, according to this faith-based system, a person who believes in Jesus and accepts the gift of the Holy Spirit doesn't have to go to the head of the church for forgiveness, blessings, or to commune with God. This leads to assurance in the Protestant faith. Assurance, sometimes referred to as the witness of the Spirit, "affirms that the inner witness of the Holy Spirit allows the Christian disciple to know that he or she is justified."

Additionally, Protestants believe that once they die, they will spend eternity in heaven. For further clarity, under the Protestant umbrella, there are several different denominations. The three main branches and a few of their subdivisions are the following:

A. Lutheranism
   a. American Association of Lutheran Churches (AALC)
   b. Apostolic Lutheran Church of America (ALCA)
   c. Association of Confessional Lutheran Churches (ACLC)
   d. Association of Free Lutheran Congregations (AFLC)

A. Anglicanism
   a. Episcopalian
   b. Baptist
   c. Methodist
   d. Pentecostal

B. Calvinism
   a. Presbyterian
   b. Reformed

This is not a complete listing but is a sample of how the larger denominations have sub denominations.

Non-Christian Religions of the East

Judaism

Jewish history begins with the covenant established between God and Abraham around 1812 BC (over 3,800 years ago) in the Middle East. The Torah (Jewish Law) is the primary document of Judaism. It was given to the Jewish people by the Prophet Moses (Moshe) about 3,300 years ago.

Judaism is one of the oldest monotheistic religions and was founded in the Middle East. Jewish people believe that God appointed them to be his chosen people in order to set an example of holiness and ethical behavior to the world.

The Jewish people have different names of God. They generally follow the names used most often in the Hebrew Bible, which are the Tetragrammaton (YHWH Hebrew: יהוה) and Elohim. Other names of God in traditional Judaism include El Shaddai and Shekhinah.

A summary of what Jewish people believe about God is that God exists, there is only one God, there are no other gods, and God can't be subdivided into different persons (unlike the Christian view of God). Jewish believers should worship only one God. God is transcendent. God doesn't have a body. God created the universe without help.

Overall, although Judaism has gone through changes as with every religious belief system, with Judaism, there is still one God, and man has no need for a savior. God has established the laws for man to follow. Overall, Jewish people believe that God wants people to do what is just and compassionate. They believe heavily in family and traditions. Judaism shares a lot of core beliefs with Christianity except for the trinary and the need for a savior. They do, however, reference two Messiahs: the son of Joseph, who would suffer and die, and the son of David, who would be a victorious king and would establish the Messianic kingdom on earth.

Islam

This religion was founded by the prophet Mohammed. Islam is in fact an Abrahamic monotheistic religion whose followers believe that Muhammad is a messenger of God. Muslims believe that the prophet Muhammad was preceded by a long succession of prophets before him that include Adam, Noah, Abraham, David, and Jesus.

The Arabic word 'Islam' is based on the root 'slam,' which means "peace or surrender to God." When one takes the whole word Islam, it means "the state of peace through following God's guidance." There are three major dimensions of Islam, which include: beliefs, ritual practices, and the effort to improve one's character and actions.

When looking at the religion of Islam, there are a series of beliefs that one must accept. They are belief in God, belief in angels, belief in God's prophets/ messengers, belief in God's revelations in the form of Holy Scriptures given to the messengers, belief in an afterlife that follows the Day of Judgment on which people will be held accountable for their actions and compensated accordingly in the afterlife, and belief in God's divine will and His (God's) knowledge of what happens in the world.

The daily practices are the profession of faith, namely that there is only one God and that Muhammad is the messenger of God. There are also the five daily prayers and required annual donation to charity in the amount of 2.5% of one's excess wealth. In addition, there is the fasting during daylight hours in the month of Ramadan and making a pilgrimage to Mecca once in a lifetime if one is mentally, physically, and financially able to do so.

Islam, as a religion, also focuses on the cultivation of excellent moral character, not only to better oneself, but also the world. With that in mind, members of the Islamic religion have an innate respect for the earth and all creatures. They show care and compassion for those less fortunate while striving continuously to improve oneself and the world. They understand the importance of seeking knowledge and interacting in honesty and truthfulness in both word and deed.

Overall, many of the critical attributes of the Islamic faith are very similar to Christianity. Many people chose to look to, denominational differences and apply them to the Islam religion holistically. However, I would caution that this kind of review with the same lens looking at Christianity would do very little to reflect the true depth of the faith.

Shintoism

Shintoism is the indigenous religion of Japan consisting chiefly in what can be considered cultic devotion to deities of natural forces and veneration of the emperor as a descendant of the sun goddess. With this, there appears to be no founder, prophets, or savior. In fact, there does not appear to be a formal doctrine with this religion. One thing for certain is the *kami*. The kami is a concept that involves gods. Shinto gods are called kami. They are sacred spirits that take the form of things and concepts important to life, such as wind, rain, mountains, trees, rivers, and fertility.

The term 'pantheistic' best represents this religion. Pantheistic actually means there is no distinction between the creator and created. Kami is actually the Japanese way of saying "the way of the gods." *Shen* means 'spirit' and *tao* means 'way.' When combined, *shen tao* means 'spirit way.'

The Shinto believe that this world is full of evil spirits, and the way of the Shinto is to gain deliverance from this cruel world. The Shinto belief has four affirmations:

- *Tradition and Family*: The family is seen as the main mechanism by which traditions are preserved.
- *Love of Nature*: Nature is sacred; to be in contact with nature is to be close to the gods. In their belief, they attribute negative behaviors to evil spirits that are present in this earth realm.
- *Death and the Afterlife*: People of the Shinto religion believe that death and the afterlife are dark and negative. Many believe that

when one dies, they will go to a dark underground realm with a river separating the living from the dead.

- *Salvation*: Overall, like the Christian, the Shinto believe that *people need salvation*. The difference arises when the Christian believes in one almighty God, and the Shinto believe in many gods in many natural things.

Confucianism

There is a big debate over whether Confucianism is a religion or an ethical philosophy of life? For the purposes of this literary work, I am going with religion, which has a very heavy emphasis on the ethical philosophy of life. This is evident because Confucius' writings and teachings placed a heavy emphasis on life on earth. He did not deal with spirits and spiritual beings, neither validating nor dismissing them. Confucianism deals a lot with ancestors and the love and respect for them.

Confucianism's foundational beliefs are that human beings are essentially good and teachable, improvable, and perfectible via personal and communal efforts. Confucianism is heavily dependent upon individuals being able to conduct honest introspective and trusting the process of self-cultivation and revitalization. Confucianism is a philosophy based on mutual respect and kindness toward others.

To be honest, Confucianism was founded prior to the birth of Confucius; however, it was developed through his later life. It gained popularity during the Han dynasty.

The main beliefs of Confucianism are xin (honesty and trustworthiness), chung (loyalty to the state, etc.), li (includes rituals, propriety, etiquette, etc.), and hsiao (love within the family, love of parents for their children, and love of children for their parents).

Overall, this religion focuses on man's ability to help himself and his society independent of a god. Again, it is not that this religion is against a deity, but just does not place their hope and trust in one as their innate belief is that man is fundamentally good.

Taoism

The individual believed to have begun Taoism was named Lao Tzu (604–517 BC). His name means "old master." It is believed that this individual was convinced to write his philosophical thoughts down as he was leaving to go on a pilgrimage. He did, and the pages were turned into a book called "Tao Te Ching (The Book of the Way)."

There is a lot of uncertainty surrounding this Chinese religion, but one thing that is for sure is the "Tao Te Ching" does exist, and it consists of eighty-one short chapters. These chapters describe the meaning of tao and how to live according to tao. For the most part, tao is translated as "way" or 'eternal path.'

This philosophical belief was given a great insurgence by one of its great Taoist philosophers, Chuang-Tzu. He did this via the development of what is now referred to as the "Taoist Canon." This canon currently consists of 1,120 volumes.

There are four main principles of Taoism that are intended to guide the relationship between humanity and nature. Taoist thought focuses on genuineness, longevity, health, immortality, vitality, *wu wei* (nonaction, a natural action, a perfect equilibrium with tao), detachment, refinement (emptiness), spontaneity, transformation, and omnipotentiality.

Taoists essentially do not think that an afterlife exists the way that many other religions do. Taoists believe that we are eternal, and that the afterlife is just another part of life itself; we are of the *tao* (the way of the natural order of the universe) when we are alive and of the *tao* when we die.

Overall, with Taoism, people are believed to possess what is needed to become good people. They must understand the difference between the 'yang' and 'yin.' After they understand the opposing forces, they can then begin to practice the good while omitting the bad. They respect nature and learn to live in ways that are harmonious with nature so as not to become destructive to an environment. Many ways and beliefs and actions of Taoist align with Christianity, except for the ideology of man being innately good! Christianity focuses on the idea that man is sinful by nature, and it is only by the grace of God that man can be redeemed.

Pseudo-Christian Religions of the West

Mormonism

Mormonism is really the religious tradition of the Latter-Day Saint movement of Restorationist Christianity started by Joseph Smith. Smith began this movement in western New York sometime around the 1820s. In the 1820s, Smith stated that he had a visitation from God the Father and God the Son. It was due to that visitation which caused him to set out and begin a church. The word 'Mormon' was originally derived from the "Book of Mormon." "The Book of Mormon" is a religious text that Smith published. In this text, he claims that he translated the information from golden plates with divine assistance. Mormons express the doctrines of Mormonism using standard biblical terminology and have similar views about the nature of Jesus' atonement, bodily resurrection, and second coming as traditional Christianity. Although their theology is similar to that of Christianity, there are some big differences.

Mormonism and Christianity have a complex theological, historical, and sociological relationship. Nevertheless, most Mormons do not accept the view that the Bible "is without error or fault in all its teaching."

Mormonism has common beliefs with the rest of the Latter-Day Saint movement, including the use of and belief in the Bible and in other religious texts, including the "Book of Mormon" and "Doctrine and Covenants." The book originally was split into two parts: a series of lectures establishing basic church doctrine, and the second part was an anthology of important "revelations" or "covenants" of the church. That is why it was referred to as the Doctrine and Covenants.

It also accepts "The Pearl of Great Price," which is a selection of choice materials touching many significant aspects of the faith and doctrine of the Church of Jesus Christ of Latter-Day Saints. These items were produced by Joseph Smith and were published in the church periodicals of his day. As part of its Scriptural canon, it has a history of teaching eternal marriage (a doctrine that marriage can last forever in heaven), eternal progression (wherein mankind can return to live in God's presence and continue as families), and polygamy (plural marriage), although the LDS Church formally abandoned the practice of plural marriage in 1890.

For Mormons, there are four levels of the afterlife:

1. *Celestial Glory* - The highest level of the celestial heavenly kingdom is for married Mormons who have kept all the celestial laws and commandments (this is what they refer to as eternal life). The lower celestial kingdom is for single Mormons who lived a worthy life and good people (including Christians) who didn't have a chance on earth to hear about and accept Mormonism. People in this lower group cannot become gods.
2. *Terrestrial Glory* - The terrestrial kingdom is for unworthy Mormons and good people who knew about Mormonism on earth but rejected it until after their death.
3. *Telestial Glory* - The telestial realm is for wicked people who rejected Mormonism even after death. They will experience suffering and pain for their sins. It's similar to the Christian version of hell, only not eternal.
4. *Hell (Outer Darkness)* - Eternal hell is for Satan, demons, and "sons of perdition" (e.g., those who deny the Holy Spirit after receiving it).

Overall, Mormons believe Joseph Smith's writings are more influential than the Bible. In addition, they deny justification by faith in Jesus Christ. However, Mormon believers do come across as orthodox believers who care for their members, including the elderly and young. They offer scouting programs and social activities and believe that everything that occurs in the church is a result of divine revelation.

Jehovah's Witnesses

Jehovah's Witnesses was founded by Charles Taze Russell (1852–1916). He was initially a member of the Congregational Church, then transferred to the beliefs of Seventh Day Adventism. It was under the latter belief system that he became known as a pastor. He was followed by Joseph Franklin Rutherford (1917), who did not make any changes to the functioning, but did embellish upon what was previously taught. Nonetheless, it was under Rutherford's lead that they actually became known as Jehovah's Witnesses. After Rutherford's time in leadership, there was Nathan Homer Knorr, the third President of the Watchtower Bible and Tract Society. The final and current leader is Frederick William Franz.

Overall, the Jehovah's Witnesses accept the portions of the Bible which they can reasonably explain. Some of their core beliefs are that they believe in God, the creator, and that Jesus Christ is his son. However, they do not believe in the Trinity, the doctrine that God, Christ, and the Holy Spirit are all aspects of one God. They base all their beliefs on the Bible as interpreted by the governing body, who produced the "Witnesses Act." They also have their own translation of the Bible called "The New World Translation."

Jehovah's Witnesses appear to be a works-based salvation system. It is their belief that their salvation is tied directly to the accomplished works that they do. Finally, they believe that Satan established the concept of the trinity and that 144,000 members will live in heaven with Christ; however, there will be "Jonadabs" who will enjoy a perfect earth forever.

Christian Science

This religious system was founded by Mary Baker Eddy. There is some confusion around the authenticity of all printed materials concerning this religious system. What is for certain is that she was a woman who suffered from some form of spinal deformity. She was married at least twice and had at least one child. She began this religious movement when she proclaimed that she was healed by the "science of health" or "Christian Science" created by Dr. Phineas Parkhurst Quimby. She began to practice what was known as Quimbyism. She actually wrote and published notes from his teaching and published manuscripts. As time went on, she married Mr. Eddy.

As Mrs. Eddy, she practiced and taught the principles of Christian Science for lots of money. She then moved on to Boston and founded the Massachusetts Metaphysical College. There, she taught for approximately nine years. As time went on, she developed a following at her Christian Science Church, so much so that by 1900, there were well over two hundred thousand followers.

In their church services, they do utilize the Bible; however, they are more inclined to follow the writings of Mary Baker Eddy. In her book "Science and Health," it utilized terms and language found in the Bible. This group believes that salvation comes about by one's discovery and awareness of their inner self. They do not believe in the deity of Jesus Christ. They believe that every experience, good or bad, is the result of illusions of the mortal mind.

Seventh-Day Adventism

This system of belief came about under the preaching of William Miller (1782–1849). He was a New York farmer who believed that the second coming of Christ was coming between March 21, 1843 and March 21, 1844. This was based on the numerology found in Daniel 8:14: "2,300 evenings and mornings." When these dates came and left, a series of other dates were proclaimed by various other followers of this belief system.

One of the most influential people in this belief system was Mrs. Ellen G. White. Her 'inspired' understanding of the Bible is believed to be "the Spirit of prophecy" (Rev. 19:10). Most of the current Seventh-Day Adventists still follow her "revelations."

Overall, this group are separatists who consider themselves to be the remnant people. They believe that they embrace an orthodox biblical position concerning many agreed-upon Christian tenants. Some of the belief systems that separate them from other 'Christian denominations' are the level of authority given to the 'inspired biblical interpretations' of Mrs. Ellen G. White. They have a level of condemnation for any other belief system that does not worship on Saturdays to the extent that it will cost them their salvation. They believe that in 1844, the record of sin was transferred to heaven to be judged by God, and when he is done, he will then cast judgment, and some will receive eternal life. The wicked will be burned alive by a great fire.

The Seventh-Day Adventists do believe in a strong education and a healthy lifestyle. They care for the people who are a part of their belief system, and they are still seeking Christ's return.

Unity School of Christianity

This belief system comes from the teachings of Phineas Parkhurst Quimby. With that being said, it shares some of the same core values of the power of the subconscious mind. Some basic background information is that Mary Baker Eddy founded the Christian Science belief system. Julius Dresser and Warren Evens were "disciples" of P. P. Quimby when he founded the New Thought cult, which leads to Myrtle Fillmore, who, upon hearing a lecture about how because she was a child of God, believed she could not get sick.

The Fillmores began to share this belief system of 'practical Christianity' via printed publications. They established a magazine that went through several name changes, from Modern Thought (1889), then Christian Science Thought (1890), then Thought (1891). In 1895, they became known as Unity.

Fillmore, a businessman, led the Unity Church Universal that was established in 1924 into many lucrative ventures. The Unity School of Christianity was one of those ventures. The Unity School of Christianity actually operates a training school, a twenty-four-hour prayer room, a broadcasting station, a vegetarian cafeteria, and a publishing company. They have merged their belief with Hinduism and mental healing. They also believe in sin, diseases, physical illnesses, and death. They borrow many terms and precepts from the Bible to establish a religious connotation.

Theosophy

Adyar is the name of a section of the Theosophical Society founded by Helena Petrovna Blavatsky and others in 1882. With her understanding of the synthesis of religion, philosophy, and science, she was able to convince people of the union with the infinite through meditation. She was believed to be an enlightened guru.

In1885, she returned to Europe, establishing the Blavatsky Lodge in London. Here she published "The Secret Doctrine," a commentary on what she said were ancient Tibetan manuscripts, as well as two additional books, "The Key to Theosophy and The Voice of the Silence." She actually leaned heavily on Buddhism and referred to angels as evolutionary products of worlds older than earth. There were not any Christian connections. They did not believe that Jesus was the Christ; actually, she stated that her son was the savior and that God is to blame for evil.

* * *

With all the faith-based systems mentioned above, what is absolutely clear is that each one began with an individual or group of individuals disagreeing with an established faith-based system. The differences may have been over abuses or differing philosophical beliefs, but what is evident is as different as each one is, they all have some form of belief in something. Proceeding with that line of thinking leads one to surmise that faith is required in each system, and there is the possibility of that faith being manipulated by the leaders.

CHAPTER 14

Survey Responses and Results

True humility is not thinking less of yourself; it's thinking of yourself less.

— C.S. Lewis

As this literary work was based on a dissertation I personally made, I would like to share with you results of the study. A survey was distributed and handed out at two different conferences. The surveys were also shared via email to people who either sent me an email or who were on my email listing. This is important, as many of the people were soliciting items, and I did not know who they were. Additionally, I requested that people share the survey with whoever they wanted, as emailing them to the return address would enhance the level of anonymity.

The multiple choice questionnaire was presented to people of differing religions, nationalities, race, genders, income levels, and philosophical ideologies. There was no targeted population. The survey consisted of thirty questions relating to the topic of metaphysical manipulation and its potential impact on people's faith. The respondents did have the option to identify themselves for a further in-depth personal interview or to remain anonymous.

The survey consisted of four sections. Each section asked several targeted questions intended to identify different thoughts and aspects of the individual surveyed. The first section looks at the demographic makeup of the individual. Next, there were some general questions around their thoughts and faith. With these questions, the individuals taking the survey were able to take a firm stance when answering the question to indicate that they are somewhere in the middle or indicate that they are not sure. Then there was a follow-up, with questions asked in which the 5-Point Likert Scale was utilized. This system was selected as it is a psychometric response system that allows the respondents to share how much they agree with particular statements.

The findings from this section provided quantitative data on the research topic. The final portion of the survey consisted of true-or-false responses. This was done to gain qualitative data pertaining to the respondent's opinions concerning faith; they either believe the statements are true or false. This information is important to the research as in a sense the respondent is requested to take a stance on the topic, there is no room in the middle. The results of the survey were reviewed and analyzed per section at first, then collectively.

Finally, a comparative analysis of what the experts have shared and what this research shows, has been done.

In addition, there will be case study reports conducted by other researchers and research studies that are not aiming to establish statistical associations between variables but a plausible association. This study also includes other related published literature.

Survey Results

The results of the survey were very interesting. Each question and statement response revealed an independent truth while collectively, groups of questions and statement responses provided insight to particular areas. With the goal of not providing opinion-based summations, following best practices of initially sharing the actual results of the survey then make any analytical presuppositions utilizing the shared data. Additionally, comparisons between the various questions and statements will occur on the page revealing the responses to each question and or statement.

The results are represented in a variety of ways. What is essential to know is that there were 181 surveys completed. When completing the surveys, the respondents were free to take the documents with them and email their responses. People were also able to complete the survey at the various locations in which it was distributed. Finally, survey takers had the option to complete the survey online. Overall, two hundred fifty (250) surveys were printed and distributed. The number of times the survey was shared via email is not available.

1) Gender (How do you Identify)
179 responses

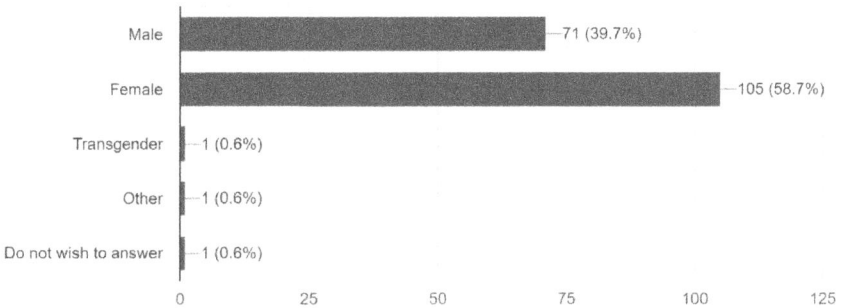

Male	71 (39.7%)
Female	105 (58.7%)
Transgender	1 (0.6%)
Other	1 (0.6%)
Do not wish to answer	1 (0.6%)

One hundred eighty-one (181) people responded, and of that number, one hundred seventy-eight (178) shared how they identified. One responded to the question with "Do not want to answer." This information is paramount to the study as 58.7% of the respondents identify as female and 39.7% male. It is not a 50-50 split, but there is a 19% point difference in the direction of females.

Additionally, the other two categories (transgender and other) represent 0.12% or 2 respondents. The interesting idea is that 179 of the participants did include a confirmed gender identity.

2) How often do you attend a religious / Spiritual service or gathering?
178 responses

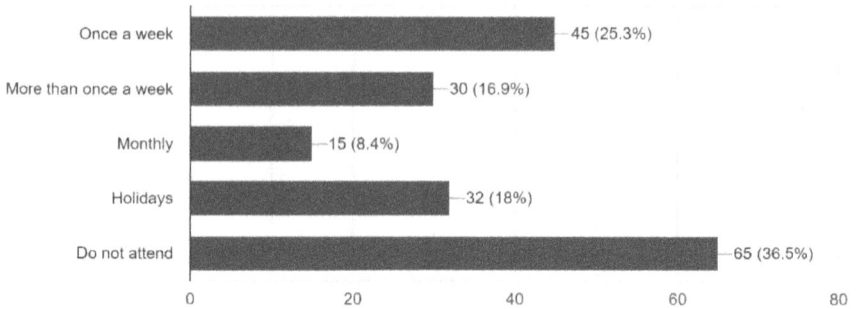

Category	Value
Once a week	45 (25.3%)
More than once a week	30 (16.9%)
Monthly	15 (8.4%)
Holidays	32 (18%)
Do not attend	65 (36.5%)

For the question concerning religious/spiritual service attendance, the data reflected some highs and lows. According to the data collected, 25.3% of the people surveyed attend some form of religious/spiritual service on a weekly basis, 16.9% attend more than once a week, and 8.4 % attend services on a monthly basis. 18% of the people indicated that they attend services/spiritual gatherings on holidays. According to this survey, approximately 68.6% of people attend services at some point while 36.5% do not attend at all. This could reflect a little over one-third of the 178 who responded; however, when reviewing the actual numbers, there were 187 responses provided, which clearly represented some overlap.

3) What are your metaphysical beliefs, do you believe in:
180 responses

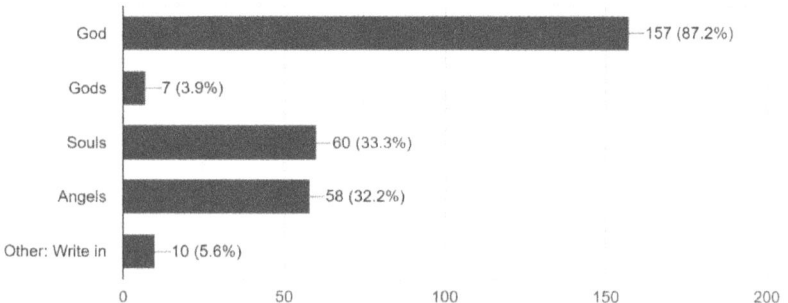

Category	Value
God	157 (87.2%)
Gods	7 (3.9%)
Souls	60 (33.3%)
Angels	58 (32.2%)
Other: Write in	10 (5.6%)

When addressing metaphysical beliefs, the participants were allowed to select multiple choices. I was a little surprised with the data. In my personal estimation, it was believed that the number of responses for God, souls, and angels would be the same. What the data shows is that there is a strong correlation between the belief in souls (60 participants) and angels (60 participants). The data does not reveal the interconnectedness of the individual's metaphysical beliefs. What it does reveal in the 157 individuals, 87.2% of the people surveyed believe in God. An actual totality of all the responses shared would be 292 responses, which indicated that it is plausible to believe that a large majority of the respondents selected God and something else, which specific combinations we cannot be certain of. Ten individuals selected others but did not share what the other was.

4) Your Religion / Belief
178 responses

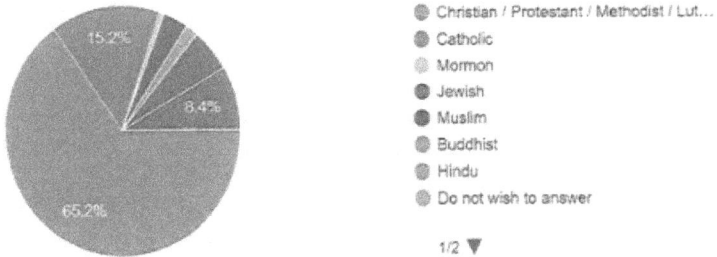

Christian / Protestant / Methodist / Lut...
Catholic
Mormon
Jewish
Muslim
Buddhist
Hindu
Do not wish to answer

1/2 ▼

When reviewing the pie chart, the largest population of individuals surveyed indicated that their religious/belief system was of the Christian persuasion (65.2%). The next largest group was Catholic with 15.2%, followed by Buddhist with 8.4%. In total, 88.8% identified with the three largest denominations. That leaves an 11.1% of respondents who vary between Jewish, Muslim, Hindu, and just did not want to answer the question. This information was disappointing to me as I was seeking a more diversified assortment of individuals. What is even more interesting is that it was believed that where I was distributing the survey and to whom they were shared with, the results would have been different. That was an assumption on my part that will not happen again.

5) Your Age
181 responses

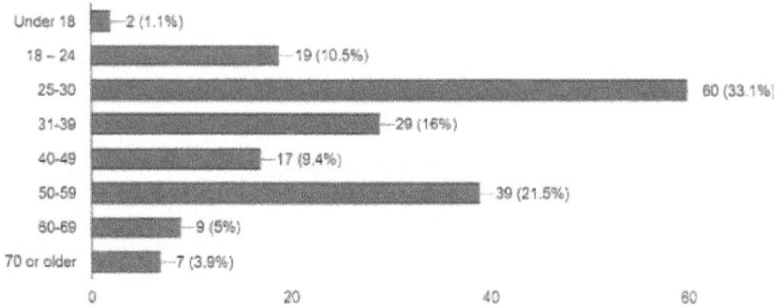

This portion of the survey was important as I wanted to ensure that a range of individuals, were given a voice in the survey. It would be interesting to see if some correlations between age and other aspects of the survey can be shared. Here we see that the largest percentage of respondents are between the ages of 25 and 30 (33.1%). For me, looking at the survey responses in total, almost every question had above a 90% response rate. It is interesting as this population of people wanted to share their voice. They provided the greatest response with one of the smallest groupings of ages (6). They are followed by the ages of 50–59 (21.5%) Just those two age groups alone make up 54.6% of the opinions shared.

The individuals between the ages of 31 and 39 came in third place as 16% of the respondents.

6) Your level of education:
181 responses

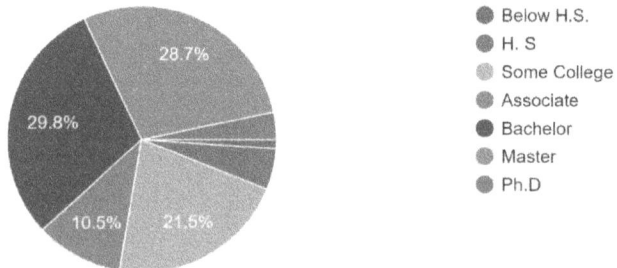

The educational attainment levels of the respondents were spread at a range that made it clear that over 90% (90.5%) of the respondents had varying college experience. It will be intriguing to see if a correlation can be made between the levels of educational attainment and the levels of church participation.

According to the pie chart, the percentages between the respondents holding a bachelor's degree (29.8%) and the respondents with a master's degree (28.7%) is not significant at all; we are looking at 1.1%. Then there are those who have some college experience (21.5%). One must not be misled by the number as some individuals may have more college credits than it would take to earn an associate degree.

These numbers appear to support the data collected concerning the respondents' ages as only two were younger than eighteen years of age.

7) Your Income level:
176 responses

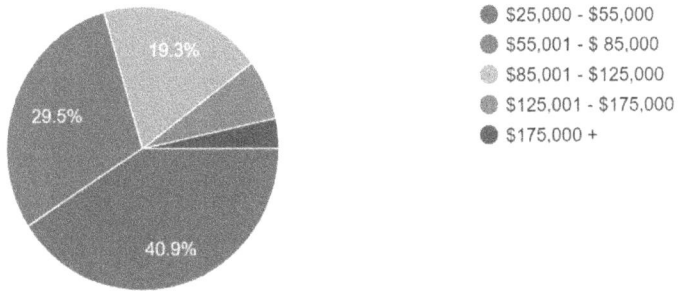

Legend:
- $25,000 - $55,000
- $55,001 - $ 85,000
- $85,001 - $125,000
- $125,001 - $175,000
- $175,000 +

Income levels were sought to see if there would be a clear correlation between income and church affiliation. What we have here is that 176 people responded to the question, which means that 5 people did not respond to the question at all. Furthermore, according to the data, the largest percentage of the respondents are in the $25,000–$50,000 range per year as their salary. The question did not specify if it was from a single or joint family income. What is also clear is that even though the $55,001–$85,000 is in second place with 29.5% of the respondents in that income bracket, there is an 11.5% gap in the income. What this also shows is 70.4% make up over half of the people surveyed. Only 19% earn between $85,001 and $125,000, but when that figure is included with the previous total, we have 89.4% of the respondents covered.

8) What do you consider faith to be?
175 responses

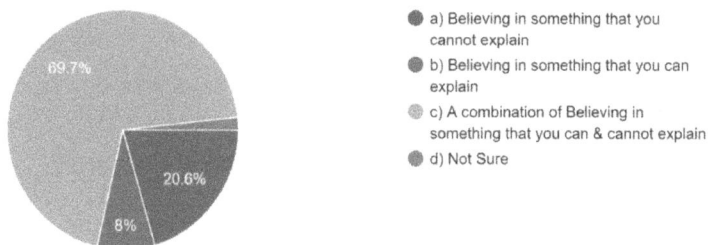

- a) Believing in something that you cannot explain
- b) Believing in something that you can explain
- c) A combination of Believing in something that you can & cannot explain
- d) Not Sure

For this question in the survey, they were given a selection to limit the possible responses. The word is very expensive in the ways in which people believe or think of faith. What was provided were a few hybrids of what the general population would consider faith to be according to my past research. To be fair, they were also provided with the option of "Not Sure."

Given the answer choices, only 175 of the people surveyed answered the question.

When asked what they consider faith to be, well over two-thirds (69.7%) of the respondents selected answer choice C, which reads, "a combination of believing in something that you can & cannot explain". 20.6% selected A, "believing in something that you cannot explain." These responses, when compared to what religion the respondents were affiliated with, 65.2% identified as Christians and 15.2% as Catholic. If we did the math, we would identify the 80.4% of the respondents were either Christian or Catholic.

9) Do you have faith in God?
176 responses

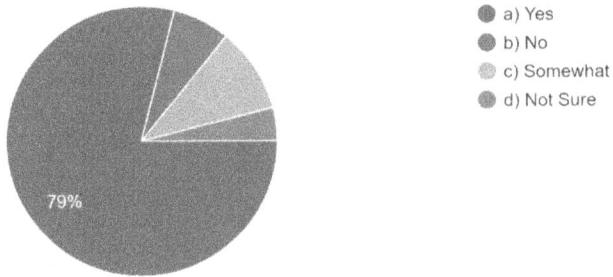

- a) Yes
- b) No
- c) Somewhat
- d) Not Sure

After answering the question "What do you consider faith to be?", it only seemed appropriate to inquire if the respondents had faith in God. This question was answered by 176 of the 181 survey takers. 79% of the people responded with "Yes." That would roughly leave about 44 in the grouping of "No," "Somewhat," and "Not Sure." Of the three, the chart shows that "Somewhat" has the largest percentage.

Working to establish a relationship between the responses is interesting as 132 individuals responded with Yes, and if we connect that to the approximately 117 who responded that faith is believing in something that you can and cannot explain, there is a definite overlap. This overlap can suggest that a great majority of those who have faith in God believe that they can both explain and not explain their faith.

10) What is the basis of your faith in God?
172 responses

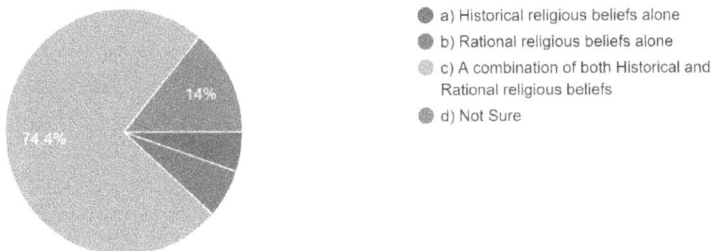

- a) Historical religious beliefs alone
- b) Rational religious beliefs alone
- c) A combination of both Historical and Rational religious beliefs
- d) Not Sure

Due to the nature of this study, it would have seemed irresponsible not to ask what is the basis of faith for those taking the survey? It seems to me when looking at this data source, the more direct or pointed the question, the fewer respondents there were. Nevertheless, in response to the question, only 172 people responded. Of that 172 people, 74.4% indicated that the basis of their faith is a combination of both historical and rational religious belief. This represents just shy of three-quarters of the responses. An additional 14% were not sure. What this says is that 15.6% are almost equally divided as to whether the basis of their faith is either rational or historical.

11) Do you believe that Absolute faith in God is realistic?
176 responses

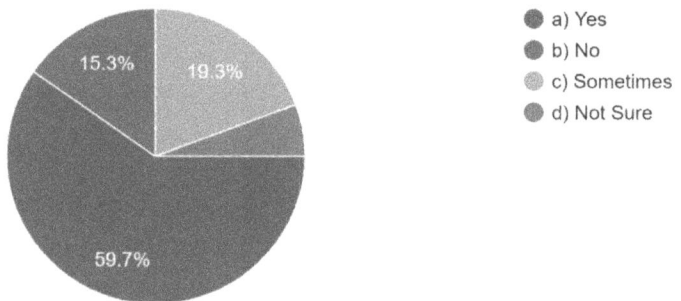

- a) Yes
- b) No
- c) Sometimes
- d) Not Sure

15.3% 19.3% 59.7%

This question was purposefully written to have the respondents share their opinion, but not necessarily indicate if that is what they believe in themselves. The reason for this is oftentimes, people are unwilling to publicly align themselves with what could be considered radical in nature.

When discussing "absolute faith" in God, that can begin to have others questing if a person truly believes in God or if they are really a member of their faith-based system. 59.7% said yes, absolute faith in God is realistic. For this question, there were more responses, 176 in total. 19.3% shared that sometimes it is possible, and 15.3 stated that it is not realistic to have absolute faith in God.

What this data source is leading toward is that although some may have faith in God, the concept of absolute faith in God is not representative of the percentage of people who say they have faith in God.

12) Do you believe that your faith can be manipulated by an individual?
175 responses

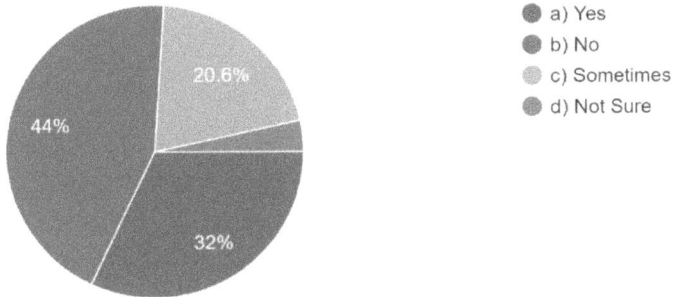

a) Yes
b) No
c) Sometimes
d) Not Sure

When asked if they believed that their faith can be manipulated, 44% of the 175 people who responded indicated no, but 32% indicated yes, and 20.0% stated sometimes. When combining the data, it appears that 52.6% of the 175 people indicated that they can be manipulated, and 3.4% were not sure. This means that in real numbers, 92.05 of the people can be manipulated, while 83 believe they cannot.

13) Do you believe that your faith can be manipulated by a religious system?
177 responses

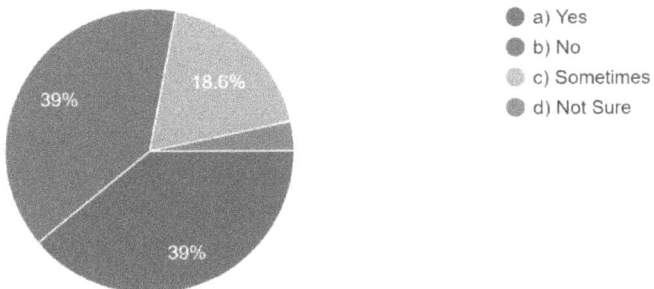

a) Yes
b) No
c) Sometimes
d) Not Sure

When considering if their faith can be manipulated by a faith-based system, there was a shift in the numbers. Immediately, it was noticed that 2 more people responded to this question than the previous one. Also, 39% of the people indicated 'No' while an even 39% of the people responded 'Yes.' Whereas with the last question about having their faith manipulated in general, 20.6% indicated sometimes, but if the manipulation was being done by a faith-based system, now 18.6% shared "Sometimes." A combination of the data leaves the same 3.4% of the 177 respondents with a "Not Sure."

So, with both questions concerning manipulation and manipulation by a faith-based system, overall, 3.4% are not sure if they can be manipulated. What is also intriguing is that there was a 2% decline when it came to being manipulated by a faith-based system over generally having one's faith manipulated.

14) Do you believe that your faith in God can be manipulated by your religious system?
174 responses

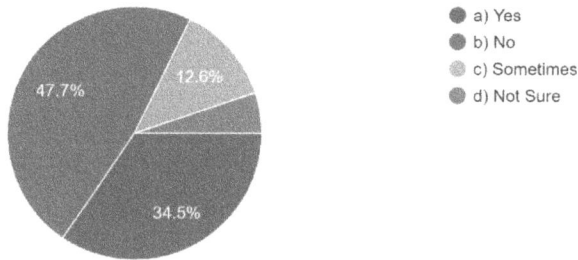

- a) Yes
- b) No
- c) Sometimes
- d) Not Sure

47.7% 12.6% 34.5%

When it was time to evaluate one's own faith-based system or religion, there was another shift. To begin with, only 174 people responded as opposed to the 177 when questioning manipulation in general by faith-based systems. Next, when looking at the number of individuals who indicated 'No,' that number increased, surpassing both of the two previous questions, "Can one's faith be manipulated?", which was 44%, and "Can one's faith be manipulated by a faith-based system?", which was 39%, to now when considering their religious system, the number moved to 47.7%. Whereas the number of people who said 'Yes' shifted down from 39% to 34.5%. The only response that stayed on a downward trajectory is the group who responded 'Sometimes,' who are now at 12.6%. Another group that showed another increase is the 'Not Sure' group. The number of respondents has increased from a staggering 3.4% to a 5.2% with 3 more people responding.

15) Do you believe that reason and evidence have an impact on your faith in God?
176 responses

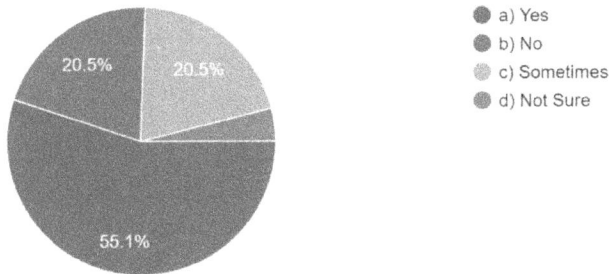

When the survey question took a shift away from systems and focused on what impacts their faith in God, the responses varied a bit. This question looked to understand what impact do reason and evidence have when it is correlated to one's faith in God. 55.1% of the individuals indicated that their faith in God is impacted by both reason and evidence, while 20.5% equally indicated 'No' and 'Sometimes.' This means that of the 176 respondents, 3.9% were not sure, which, when rounded, equals 7 people (according to the percentages, it would leave 6.86%).

This is interesting because when asked in question number 10, "What is the basis of your faith?" 74.4% responded with a combination of rational and historical beliefs, whereas less than 15% indicated that their faith was based on rational beliefs.

16) Do you believe that people should have to justify their faith in God?
177 responses

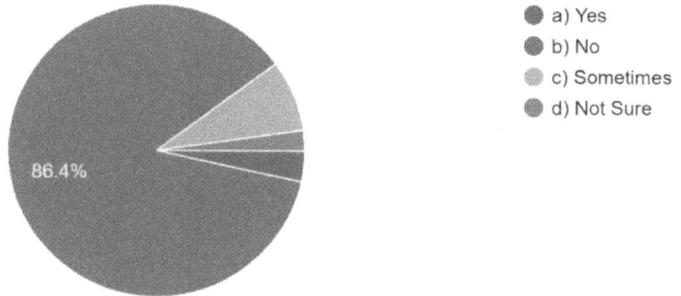

● a) Yes
● b) No
◉ c) Sometimes
● d) Not Sure

86.4%

Justification is included in this survey as a means to see if justifying one's faith would lead to faith by works or by acceptance. The overwhelming percentage of those surveyed indicated "No"-- 86.4% of those who responded do not believe that people should have to justify their faith in God. This leaves 13.6% of the respondents in the class of either 'Sometimes,' 'Yes,' or 'Not Sure.'

17) There, has been a breach in the trust placed in faith-based leadership (organized religion).
177 responses

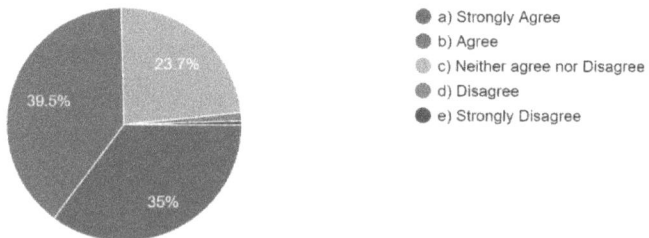

● a) Strongly Agree
● b) Agree
◉ c) Neither agree nor Disagree
● d) Disagree
● e) Strongly Disagree

23.7%
39.5%
35%

With this portion of the survey, the focus has shifted from the respondents to faith-based leaders. More specifically, this question is looking to see the individual's level of agreement as it relates to a breach in trust placed in faith-based leadership. What the pie chart shows is that 35% of the 177 people strongly agree while 39.5% agree. Based on this data alone, almost three-quarters (74.5%) believe on some level that there has been a breach in the trust placed in faith-based leadership.

What was odd was the notion that 23.7% did not agree or disagree with the statement. There were very few individuals who disagreed on any level that there had been a breach in the trust placed in faith-based leadership, approximately 1.8%.

When looking at this data, one could begin to consider how trusting on average are the local congregations and people holistically of faith-based leadership if such a large percentage believe there has been a breach.

18) The relationship between metaphysics and religion does impact faith.
176 responses

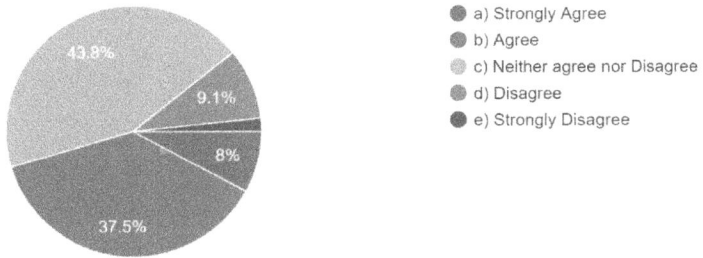

- a) Strongly Agree
- b) Agree
- c) Neither agree nor Disagree
- d) Disagree
- e) Strongly Disagree

When asked about metaphysics and religion, a number of the respondents did inquire what is meant by the term 'metaphysics.' The definition of metaphysics as utilized by this research was on the top of the survey as a term to know. The shared definition of metaphysics is "the branch of philosophy that examines the fundamental nature of reality, including the relationship between mind and matter, between substance and attribute, and between potentiality and actuality, dealing with what 'is' outside of the physical world with a focus on Souls, Angels, God, Gods and Spirits."

The responses to this survey statement, were as follows:

1. 43.8% Neither Agreed or Disagreed
2. 37.5% Agreed
3. 9.1% Disagreed
4. 8% Strongly Agreed
5. 1.6% Strongly Disagreed

As a number of physical respondents wrestled with the term *metaphysics*, it led to the understanding that respondents who were not present were not privy to the same understanding of the term and may, on some level, render these responses as questionable.

It should be noted that the largest percentage of respondents, 43.8%, did not agree or disagree. This for the basis of interpretive analysis would lead one to believe that the information provided in totality is very reflective of the respondents' true beliefs and opinions.

19) People should have to justify their faith in God.
176 responses

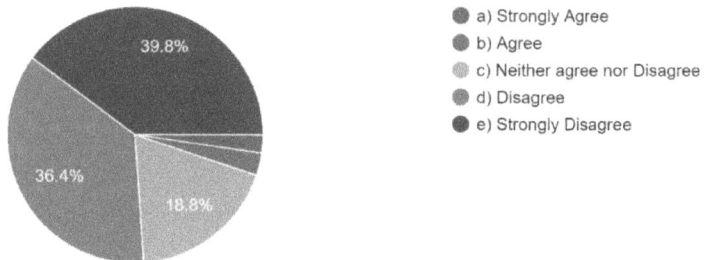

The statement concerning justifying one's belief in God is a repeat of a former question. The reasoning behind this statement is to compare its alignment with the responses to survey question number 16, which asks, "Do you believe that people should have to justify their faith in God?"

As a reminder, the responses to question number 16 were that 86.4% indicated "No." This was out of 177 responses.

As for this statement, 39.8% strongly disagreed, 36.4% disagreed, and 18.9% neither agreed nor disagreed. When looking at the results for some level of agreement, 14.9% of the respondents fell into this category.

When a comparison is made between the statement and the question, what the data shows is that when asked that question, "Should people have to justify their faith?", the response was a solid 86.4% 'No,' but when presented as a statement, the responses of 'No' had dwindled to 76.2%, which represents about a 10% decline. But when it relates to 'Yes,' 'Not Sure,' and 'Sometimes,' that represented 13.6%, and for the statement, 14.9% agreed, which represented a greater percentage than when posed as a question. For the statement of people having to justify their faith, 18.9% indicated that they 'Neither Agreed nor Disagreed,' which was much greater than the response to question 16's 'Not Sure.'

20) There are external factors (out of our realm of physical knowledge) which are really guiding people's thinking and behavior.
175 responses

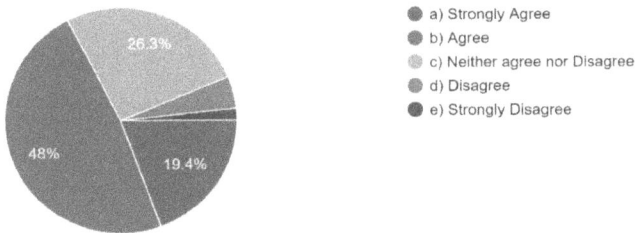

a) Strongly Agree
b) Agree
c) Neither agree nor Disagree
d) Disagree
e) Strongly Disagree

Stating that there are external factors (out of this realm of physical knowledge) that are really guiding people's thinking and behavior, this questioned if the respondents believed that people are, in essence, being led by something other than reason and evidence. This statement is in relation to number 15, which asked, "Do you believe that reason and evidence have an impact on your faith?"

What the data shows is that 48% of the responses agreed with the statement that there are external factors (out of this realm of physical knowledge) that are really guiding people's thinking and behavior. In addition to those who agreed, 19.4% strongly agree. However, 26.3% of the respondents neither agreed nor disagreed with the statement. That left 6.3% of the respondents who either disagreed or strongly disagreed.

What is shown here is that while 55.1% believed their faith was guided by reason and evidence, the same respondents shared that 74.3% also believe that external factors outside this realm of physical knowledge are controlling their thinking. However, if one were to connect the "Yes" responses and the "Sometimes" responses from question 15, you would have 75.6%, which is more in alignment with question 21's 74.3%.

21) There is something (Religious impartation) inside of people guiding their thoughts and behavior.
175 responses

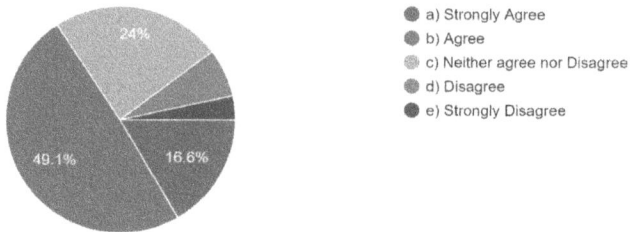

- a) Strongly Agree
- b) Agree
- c) Neither agree nor Disagree
- d) Disagree
- e) Strongly Disagree

Religious impartation is somewhat in alignment with question number 20's statement, that there are external factors (out of this realm of physical knowledge) that are really guiding people's thinking and behavior. Again, slight shifts in the questions or statements were utilized to see how the respondents thought about where their faith-based beliefs are coming from.

According to this statement, there is something (religious impartation) inside of people guiding their thoughts and behavior. 49.1% of the 175 responses strongly agreed with the statement. Another 16.6% agreed, whereas 24% neither agreed nor disagreed with the statement concerning religious impartation and its guiding individuals' thoughts and behaviors. With a summation of the data, the remaining statements' responses, disagree and strongly disagree, are at 10.3%.

When compared with question number 20 concerning external factors out of this physical realm influencing/guiding people's thinking and behavior, there was a response in the area of agreement at 67.4%, but in comparison to the consideration of religious impartations, the response in the area of agreement was 65.7%. What was interesting was the similarity between those who strongly agreed. When considering external factors out of this realm, 49% agreed, and when considering religious impartation, 49.1% agreed.

The decline came with the respondents who strongly agreed—19.4% strongly agreed with the external influential factor, and 16.6% strongly agreed with the religious impartation influencing thinking and behavior. With both statements, there was a relatively significant number of responses that indicated that they neither agreed nor disagreed with the statements. Statement number 20 had 26.3%, and question 21 had 24%.

22) People are autonomous and are not guided by any "Faith Based" system of beliefs.
174 responses

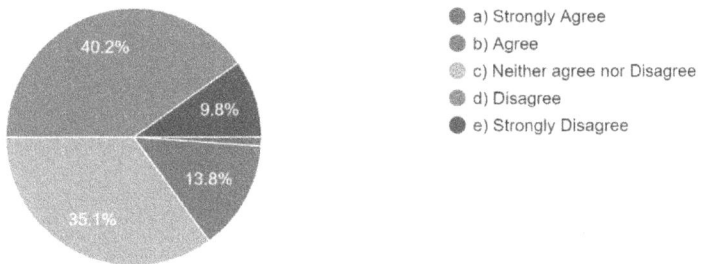

People's autonomy was questioned or challenged with statement number 22. The purpose behind this statement was to understand if the responses would lean in the direction of individuals being guided or directed by faith-based systems. This type of dialogue had to continually be held or proposed in order to identify if faith-based systems are manipulating people. This question looks at whether people consider whether or not they are being manipulated by a faith-based system.

Well, 174 individuals responded to this question. The pie chart reflects the following results. Only 1.1% of the respondents strongly agree with the statement that people are autonomous and are not guided by any faith-based system of beliefs. The largest response was to option C, which indicates a disagreement with the statement.

This is one of the areas where almost half of the respondent's showed disagreement. A little over a third of the responses reflect that they neither agreed nor disagreed with the statement, while 13.8% agreed with the autonomy of people. Overall, according to the survey results, 14.9% of the responses were in favor of the idea that people live autonomously.

23) Metaphysics, Religion and Faith are connected.
177 responses

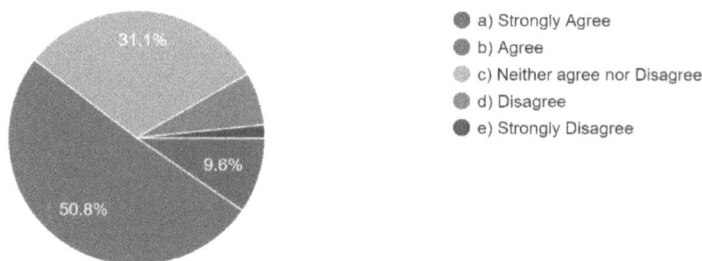

a) Strongly Agree
b) Agree
c) Neither agree nor Disagree
d) Disagree
e) Strongly Disagree

In statement 23, metaphysics, religion, and faith are now placed together. At this point in the survey, the respondents have responded to multiple questions and statements concerning faith, religion, and metaphysics.

The individuals' responses to the statement were 31.1% of the respondents did not agree or disagree. When these results were revealed, they did not closely resemble the portion of individuals who responded to a similar statement when they needed to consider how they felt about the relationship between metaphysics and religion and whether or not it impacts one's faith. That was statement 18. Actually, the response of 'Neither Agree nor Disagree' had the greatest percentage with 43.8%.

It was interesting to note that 50% of the people agreed with the statement, and 9.6% strongly agreed to the connectedness of metaphysics, faith, and religion. When comparing this to the previous time that metaphysics was mentioned in the survey, 45.5% agreed to the connection, which is 14.1% lower. With that being shared, around 10% disagreed with the connection in statement 18 while in statement 23, 8.4% disagreed to some extent.

24 Faith is taught
176 responses

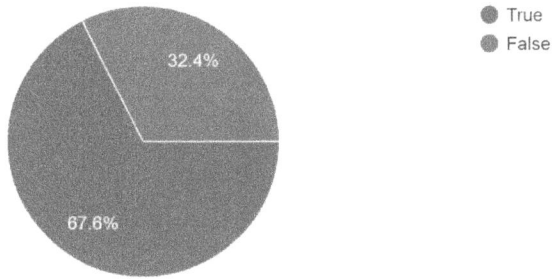

67.6% of the 176 responses reflect the opinion that faith is taught, while 32.4% believe the statement to be false.

25 Faith is irrational
175 responses

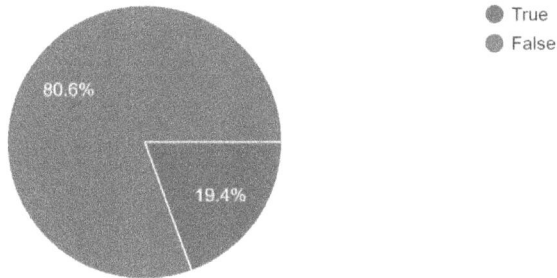

The larger percentage of the 175 responses disagree with the statement that faith is irrational, whereas 19.4% think the statement is true.

26 Explanations and Evidence increase one's faith
177 responses

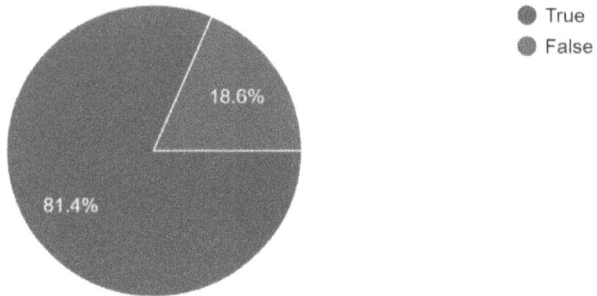

True
False

18.6%

81.4%

Of the 177 responses, 81.4% believe this statement to be true while 18.4% think it to be false.

27 Faith can be explained
176 responses

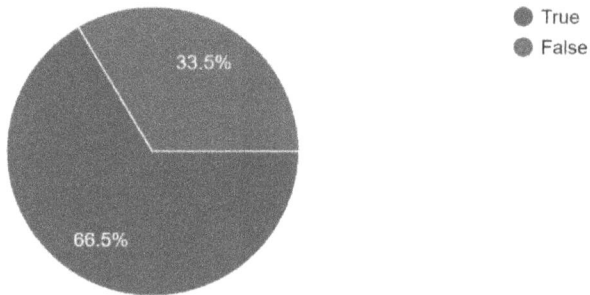

True
False

33.5%

66.5%

Well, over half of the 176 responses to the statement agreed, at 66.5%, and this reflects two-thirds of the people. 33.5% find the statement to be false.

28 Faith alone is necessary to hold religious beliefs
177 responses

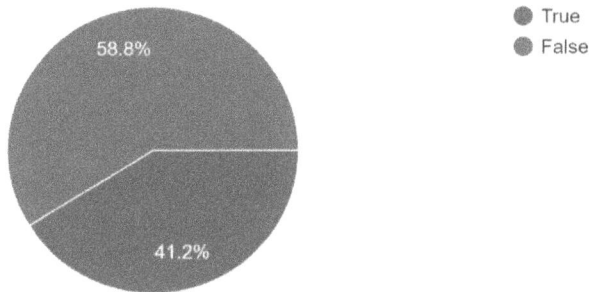

● True
● False

58.8%

41.2%

When it came time to consider the necessity of faith alone as a requirement in relation to holding religious beliefs, the responses were close. Actually, 58.8% of the 177 responses share that they believed the statement above to be false. That left 41.2% in agreement with the statement.

29 Faith alone is necessary to practice religious rites and rituals
177 responses

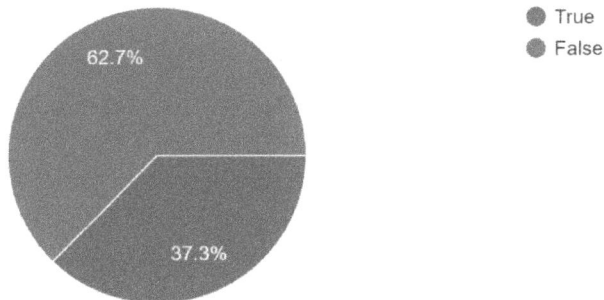

● True
● False

62.7%

37.3%

To stretch the thoughts of survey takers a little further, we considered rites and rituals. The 177 individuals who responded, almost two-thirds (62.7%) thought that the statement above is false. On the other hand, 37.3% agreed that faith alone is necessary to practice religious rites and rituals.

30 Faith can exist without Evidence or Explanation.
177 responses

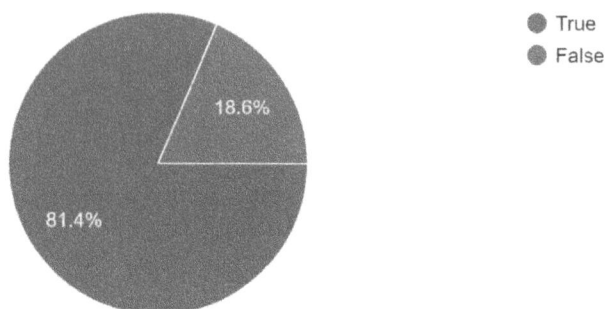

- True
- False

18.6%

81.4%

When given to answer the question directly concerning faith, 81.4% responded that faith can exist without evidence or explanation. The remaining 18.6% disagreed and indicated that the statement was false.

Thank you for your thoughts!
17 responses

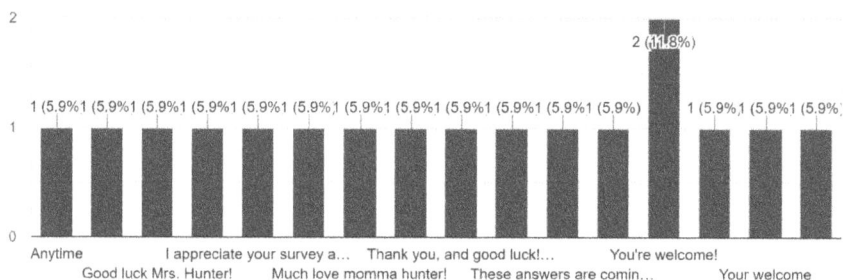

2 (11.8%)

1 (5.9%)1 (5.9%)1 (5.9%)1 (5.9%)1 (5.9%)1 (5.9%)1 (5.9%)1 (5.9%)1 (5.9%)1 (5.9%)1 (5.9%)1 (5.9%)   1 (5.9%)1 (5.9%)1 (5.9%)

Anytime   I appreciate your survey a...   Thank you, and good luck!...   You're welcome!
    Good luck Mrs. Hunter!   Much love momma hunter!   These answers are comin...   Your welcome

At the end of the survey, the respondents were allowed to share any further thought or opinion concerning any of the thirty questions above. There are a total of 22 responses, as recorded below:

1. This was a really well-done survey!
2. Faith can be explained if necessary. Faith is based on personal relationship rather than "religion."
3. Faith is derived from going through real world experiences and getting through the worst of time even when in the thick of things, you thought you could not.

4. You can have faith in many situations without needing evidence or explanations as long as you alone believe the virtues of your faith.

5. I think all the questions on faith is relative to the individual person. People's upbringing, circumstances, and religious beliefs determine level, or lack of faith in a particular stance. God-Science— or that there's nothing out there at all.

6. I believe that faith is a further development of our ability to trust, and when our trust is broken our faith and our ability to have faith is cut off. In this absence we are forced to focus on only what is outside of us, rather than inside of us.

7. I believe that others faith can be manipulated but not mine. I also believe that others faith can be manipulated by a religious system but not mine.

8. Hebrews 11:1.

9. Faith is a belief that I feel had more to do with a person's experiences in life, and less with religious factors. One is more likely to have faith of there's evidence of how having faith had a positive impact on their lived experiences.

10. The definition of faith is ambiguous and thus implicates ones idea of faith in "X." Faith is, according to ones definition, malleable and thus impacts survey submission. Day to day things chance so the questions, in my mind, should be better designed.

11. Wishing you all the best.

12. These questions make you think!

13. Baptized Catholic but my belief system is Nothing in Particular.

14. I believe that there is some higher power that helps guide our decisions and actions, but that being a God does not fit into my ideals. My one big conflict theory is that if God created everything on this Earth, then who created God? I also do believe in soul survival, that when we die we connect with certain people so deeply because we may have known them in a past life.

15. Religion and faith come from (in my opinion) how you are introduced to it. Growing up with it as a system of repetitive action for worship plays a roll in an individuals beliefs and faults

as they age. Faith CAN be separated from religion, but I do believe that they are rooted the same.

16. My religious system is other.

17. Blind faith is a type of faith.

18. I attend religious services for family masses.

19. Faith is a choice and God allows us choices, its up to us what we do with it.

20. We all have the same faith no matter what higher being we believe in or religion we practice. All of our religions or spiritual beliefs are the same.

21. Although I am not a religious-person, but I do acknowledge the power & reality of faith as a mechanism for finding a guiding truth for how they conduct their lives. Just because it is not my truth does not mean I cannot see why it is their truth.

22. I don't feel like faith has to be necessarily be taught. I think it is something you can also experience. I do feel like metaphysics can affect your view & outlook. One reason when both are combined and have an impact on your faith if you are highly gullible & impressionable. I do feel like metaphysics, religion and faith are connected, depending upon how you view the world.

This portion of the survey is just as important as the survey items. It is essential to hear from the people responding in their own voice. The takeaways are thought-provoking and engaging. One shared thought, "Faith is a choice, and God allows us choices. It's up to us what we do with it." This response caught my attention as it almost aligns itself to that of the metaphysical Christians reviewed earlier in this book.

CHAPTER 15

Conclusions and Implications

Terms can be used interchangeably, though they are not synonymous, to lead people to come up with misleading hypothetical beliefs based on a manipulation of those terms.

— Kim Spivey-Hunter

As I ponder this book and the research behind it, there is a realization of the impact of 1 Corinthians 13 in its totality. However, for this moment in time, please read 1 Corinthians 13: 9–12 (NKJV):

For we know in part, and we prophesy in part.

But when that which is perfect is come, then that which is in part shall be done away.

When I was a child, I spake as a child, I understood as a child, I thought as a child: but when I became a man, I put away childish things.

For now we see through a glass, darkly; but then face to face: now I know in part; but then shall I know even as also I am known.

From here I return to a previous thesis written in 2019 entitled "Nouthetic Counseling: Can It Produce a Spiritual Transformation?" Let us further reflect on a portion of that writing, which reads as follows:

The authors of "Christ Centered Therapy," actually quoted David Noebel. "Trying to separate the sacred from the secular is like trying to sear the soul from the body—a deadly experiment. We must recognize that all worldviews have religious implications."

I would venture to state that what is seen as socially acceptable or unacceptable gains its historical stance from a society's religious beliefs and practices. That is why in some areas, polygamy is socially acceptable and in others it is not. We can also say the same thing about the cow. In some areas, the cow is seen as a hearty meal source, and in others, the cow is a sacred animal. This comparison can stretch and go on for some time; nonetheless, that will have to wait until a sociological study of Christian Psychology is conducted and written about.

I am reminded of the scripture in the book of James 1. As I will be pulling various verses of scriptures from this chapter alone, it is important to understand what James was addressing in this very first chapter.

James was reminding some and warning others of who God is and who they are in Him. From reading the very first chapter of the book of James, he makes it abundantly clear that there will be a trying of one's faith. James 1:3 (NKJV) states, "Knowing this, that the trying of your faith worketh patience," but they need to understand who is trying or testing their faith. James 1:13 (NKJV) goes on to say, "Let no man say when he is tempted, I am tempted of God: for God cannot be tempted with evil, neither tempteth he any man."

It was and is imperative that all believers understand that as they are new and young to the 'faith,' they do not have all of the answers.

That being said, they have access to "One" who does. James 1:5 (NKJV) shares, "If any of you lack wisdom, let him ask of God, that giveth to all men liberally, and upbraideth not; and it shall be given him." But nevertheless, to continue with the works of the Lord, not to be saved but because they are saved, verse 27 reads, "Pure religion and undefiled before God and the Father is this: To visit the fatherless and widows in their affliction, and to keep himself unspotted from the world." Furthermore in his writing, James was swiftly transparent in his surmising of who he was and who he is representing in this writing. James 1:1 (NKJV) reads, "James, a servant of God and of the Lord Jesus Christ, to the twelve tribes which are scattered abroad, greeting."

Again this chapter of James as written in the King James Version of the Bible was shared, it superimposes the very notion that our faith will be tried and tested. It is also placed here to encourage the idea that if a person's faith is being manipulated/tried, who is the actual manipulator?

What has been identified and explained as manipulation, if one is not careful, can be seen by others as care, concern, and providing guidance. However, a closer look will reveal how in many religions, the religious leaders are utilizing metaphysic manipulation to impact people's faith. When considering the thirteen forms of manipulation with a careful eye, they are all present within the various faith-based religious systems reviewed in a previous chapter.

This is where epistemology has to be reintroduced. Epistemology is the part of philosophy that engages in questioning a person's deeply held beliefs and further shows by way of reason what can and can't be justified. However, when addressing faith in its purest form of meaning, it has to be considered: "If there is a way to reason one into believing or doing anything, then absolute faith is not in operation." So when this question arises, "Has metaphysical manipulation impacted people's faith?" if considering absolute faith, the answer is *no*! Why? Again, absolute faith cannot be explained or justified. There is no reason or rationale that can explain this form of faith, which would further indicate that there was nor is any way to manipulate it.

Although many people indicate that they have absolute faith, as was shared previously, there are what has been termed 'affective component of faith,' which read as "faith as knowledge, faith and reason: the epistemology of faith, faith as belief, faith as trust, faith as doxastic venture, faith as sub- or non-doxastic venture, faith and hope, faith as a virtue, and faith beyond (Orthodox) theism." When considering these components of faith, evidentialism is clearly a major contributor.

Evidentialism is broadly utilized throughout the Church age. Consider this from the Catholic Church. Until recent times, women were not allowed to be ordained priests of churches. This was and is primarily the stance in both Catholic and Orthodox Christian faith-based systems. As per the Catholic faith, priests are to represent the "likeness of Jesus," a male figure. Because priests are supposed to represent the likeness of Jesus, then women cannot represent Christ the male figure.

In 1995, the then pope wrote a letter to women everywhere, stating, "The presence of a certain diversity of roles is in no way prejudicial to women, provided that this diversity is not the result of an arbitrary imposition, but is rather an expression of what is specific to being male and female." As was shared earlier, the Pope is almost as revered as Jesus.

We can consider some historical accusations of mental manipulation against a religious system accused of deceiving the people and taking full advantage of them mentally, emotionally, and morally. Consider when John Wycliff nailed what he titled the "Twelve Conclusions" to the doors of both St. Paul's Cathedral and Westminster Abbey. This action took place after he presented his concerns to the Parliament of England, attacking what he considered to be corruption taking place in the churches.

John Wycliff established the rewriting of the Bible into an English translation. He is considered one of the forerunners of the Protestant Reformation. He did have a following who no longer believed or had faith in what the Catholic Church and the Eastern Orthodox churches were teaching. Thus the Lollards faith-based belief system began.

Consider "The Ninety-Five Theses" written and shared by Martin Luther. As a professor of moral theology, he studied and researched manipulation of faith-based leadership. It was in fact his studies that led him to write, present, and share with everyone who would take "The Ninety-Five Theses." One of the things addressed in the writing is the selling of plenary indulgences. Martin Luther stood firmly against the mental and spiritual manipulation of people.

With the enlightenment writings, preaching, and teachings of the individuals that led to the Protestant Reformation, it would be considered that with this newer, more enlightened body of faith believers that one would be able to emphatically proclaim that there is no longer any metaphysical manipulation of individuals' faith. However, what research and history has shared is that with the shift to Protestantism, metaphysical manipulation of people's faith at the hands of faith-based leaders has continued to flourish. It is important to reiterate at this juncture that manipulation may not necessarily fully implicate negativity, but it does indicate the causing of a shift in a person's faith-based beliefs by a religious leader due to their own personal objections and for the perpetuation of their opinion.

This manipulation is seen time and time again. John Edwards was considered by many as a leader in the area of metaphysics and theology and was able to shift the thinking and faith-based beliefs of millions. According to an article written by Ray Tyler entitled "Jonathan Edwards: Founding Father of American Evangelicalism," he shared that "it is believed by historians that John Edwards 'provided pre-revolutionary America with a radical, even democratic, social and political ideology.' He is considered to have begun the 'New Awakening.'"

Roger Williams is considered to have been the father of the Baptist faith-based church in America. Williams was against some of the extreme or manipulative proponents of the Congregationalist assemblies and was actually thrown out of the faith. He began the Baptist faith-based belief system. As he sought to be ecumenical, he welcomed all believers, seeking to identify what brought them together and not what segregated them. Even with these arms-outstretched beginnings, there was a split within the Baptist faith due to metaphysical manipulation of the leadership. The one became two, and they were referred to as Separatists and General Baptists.

As the shift is made to conclude this writing, the following portion is included to aid in the final summation of thought.

"It has often been considered, who wrote the Bible? Christianity is one of the only belief systems to which there is no 'human contribution as the beginner or founder of the faith.' Furthermore, this faith-based system then goes on to tell individuals that they are "sinners" to begin with and that the only way to act in any "good" way is via the help of the Holy Spirit. Christians are striving for perfection, to which they can never achieve in this lifetime, so they must settle for the constant chastisement and berating of 'Christian Leaders,' who also according to the Christian faith *are* sinners by nature."

—Author Unknown

Let's consider Dr. Harriet Braiker. Dr. Braiker was a clinical and social psychologist, a best-selling author, and a known and respected expert concerning issues impacting women. In one of her best-selling books, "Who's Pulling Your Strings? How to Break the Cycle of Manipulation and Regain Control of Your Life," Dr. Braiker wrote the following quote:

If you are an approval addict, your behavior is as easy to control as that of any other junkie. All a manipulator needs to do is a simple two-step process: Give you what you crave, and then threaten to take it away. Every drug dealer in the world plays this game.

—Harriet B. Braiker

What makes this so interesting is the sheer notion that people are seeking the approval of other people, sometimes over the written and expressed will of God.

With all things considered, I must reasonably conclude that *yes*, metaphysical manipulation by faith-based leadership has influenced people's faith.

Here's my final thought:

The problem with today's world is that everyone believes they have the right to express their opinion *and* have others listen to it. The correct statement of individual rights is that everyone has the right to an opinion, but crucially, that opinion can be roundly ignored and even made fun of, particularly if it is demonstrably nonsense!

—Brian Cox

GLOSSARY

Agential Capacities. These capacities are interrelated, but can be loosely grouped under the headings of "self-improvement," "exerting control," and "identifying patterns and achieving goals."

Agential Cuts. This refers to the cutting together/apart within phenomena. Agential cuts are momentary stabilizations, doings rather than beings. They enact that which is inside and outside of phenomena in a single movement.

Analytic Propositions. Analytic propositions are true or not true solely by virtue of their meaning.

Anthropocentric. This idea regards humankind as the central or most important element of existence, especially as opposed to God or animals.

Anthropocentrism. This idea regards humans as separate from and superior to nature and holds that human life has intrinsic value while other entities (including animals, plants, mineral resources, and so on) are resources that may justifiably be exploited for the benefit of humankind.

Biblical Apocrypha. This pertains to the collection of apocryphal ancient books thought to have been written sometime between 200 BC and AD 400. The traditional eighty-book Protestant bibles include fourteen books in an intertestamental section between the Old Testament and New Testament called the Apocrypha, deeming these useful for instruction but are noncanonical.

Catholic Moral Theology. This is a major category of doctrine in the Catholic Church equivalent to religious ethics. Moral theology encompasses Catholic social teaching, Catholic medical ethics, sexual ethics, and various doctrines on individual moral virtue and moral theory. It can be distinguished as dealing with "how one is to act" in contrast to dogmatic theology, which proposes "what one is to believe."

Canonical. This refers to ideas, thoughts, or beliefs according to or ordered by canon law.

Congregationalism. This emphasizes the right and responsibility of each properly organized congregation to determine its own affairs without having to submit these decisions to the judgment of any higher human authority. As such, it eliminates bishops and presbyteries. Each individual church is regarded as independent and autonomous, with the theological position somewhere between Presbyterianism and the more radical Protestantism of the Baptists and Quakers.

Consubstantiation. This is a Christian theological doctrine that, like transubstantiation, describes the real presence of Christ in the Eucharist. It holds that during the sacrament, the substance of the body and blood of Christ are present alongside the substance of the bread and wine, which remain present. It was part of the doctrines of Lollardy and considered a heresy by the Roman Catholic Church. It was later championed by Edward Pusey of the Oxford Movement and is therefore held by many high-church Anglicans.

Contemporary Philosophy. This refers to the present period in the history of Western philosophy beginning at the early twentieth century with the increasing professionalization of the discipline and the rise of analytic and continental philosophy.

Cosmological. This relates to the origin and development of the universe.

Curmudgeonly (especially of an old person). This term refers to someone bad-tempered and negative.

Dead Sea Scrolls. These are ancient Jewish and Hebrew religious manuscripts that were found in the Qumran Caves in the Judaean Desert near Ein Feshkha on the northern shore of the Dead Sea in the West Bank. These are the last discovered scrolls found in the Cave of Horror in Israel. Most of the texts are written on parchment, some on papyrus, and one on copper.

Deuterocanonical Books. These are books and passages considered by the Catholic Church, the Eastern Orthodox Church, the Oriental Orthodox Churches, and the Assyrian Church of the East to be canonical books of the Old Testament. However, Protestant denominations do not regard these as part of the biblical canon.

Divine Command Theory. This is a meta-ethical theory that proposes that an action's status as morally good is equivalent to whether or not it is commanded by God.

Doctrine of Assumption. The Catholic Church has two different traditions concerning the assumption/dormition of Mary. In the first, she rose from the dead after a brief period and then ascended into heaven; in the second, she was "assumed" bodily into heaven before she died.

Dogma. In a broad sense, this refers to any belief held unquestioningly and with undefended certainty, usually combined with sectarianism.

Dogmatic. This is the strong expression of opinions as if they were facts.

Domain of Discourse. In predicate logic, this is an indication of the relevant set of entities that are being dealt with by quantifiers. This is also the set of entities over which certain variables of interest in some formal treatment may range.

Deontological Ethics. This refers to when an action is considered morally good because of some characteristic of the action itself, not because the product of the action is good. Deontological ethics holds that at least some acts are morally obligatory regardless of their consequences for human welfare.

Doxastic Voluntarism. This is the philosophical doctrine according to which people have voluntary control over their beliefs.

Ecumenical. This term relates to or represents the whole of a body of churches. This is also used to promote or tend toward worldwide Christian unity or cooperation. It is worldwide or general in extent, influence, or application.

Empiricism. This is a theory that states that knowledge comes only or primarily from sensory experience. Historically, empiricism was associated with the "blank slate" concept (tabula rasa), according to which the human mind is "blank" at birth and develops its thoughts only through experience.

Epistemic Constructivism. This is a view in philosophy according to which all "knowledge is a compilation of human-made constructions."

Epistemic Idealism. This is a broad term referring to both an ontological view about the world being in some sense mind-dependent and a corresponding epistemological view that everything we know can be reduced to mental phenomena.

Epistemic Relativism. This is the view that what is true, rational, or justified for one person need not be true, rational, or justified for another person. Epistemic relativists therefore assert that while there are relative facts about truth, rationality, justification, and so on, there is no perspective-independent fact of the matter.

Epistemological. This term relates to the theory of knowledge, especially in regard to its methods, validity, scope, and the distinction between justified belief and opinion. "What epistemological foundation is there for us."

Epistemology. This is the branch of philosophy concerned with knowledge. Epistemologists study the nature, origin, and scope of knowledge, epistemic justification, the rationality of belief, and various related issues.

Erudition. This refers to quality of having or showing great knowledge or learning. Also defined as scholarship.

Etymological. This relates to the origin and historical development of words and their meanings.

Etymological Fallacy. This pertains to a genetic fallacy that holds that the present-day meaning of a word or phrase should necessarily be like its historical meaning.

Euthyphro Dilemma. This is found in Plato's dialogue Euthyphro, in which Socrates asks Euthyphro, "Is the pious [τὸ ὅσιον] loved by the gods because it is pious, or is it pious because it is loved by the gods?"

Evidentialism. This term implies that full religious belief is justified only if there is conclusive evidence for it.

Faith. This relates to the inner attitude, conviction, or trust relating human beings to a supreme god or ultimate salvation. In religious traditions stressing divine grace, it is the inner certainty or attitude of love granted by God himself.

Fallacy. This is the use of invalid or otherwise faulty reasoning or "wrong moves" in the construction of an argument. A fallacious argument may be deceptive by appearing to be better than it really is.

Fallibilism. This is the philosophical claim that no belief can have justification that guarantees the truth of the belief or that no beliefs are certain.

Feigning Ignorance. This is the act of pretending not to recognize (somebody). Feigning ignorance is an effective tactic that manipulates the person confronting the behavior into having doubts about the legitimacy of the issue they're trying to bring to the other person's attention. It can cause a person to question their sanity.

Fiducial Model. This is a model of faith as trust, understood not simply as an affective state but as an action.

First-Order Logic. This is a collection of formal systems used in mathematics, philosophy, linguistics, and computer science. First-order logic uses quantified variables over no-logical objects and allows the use of sentences that contain variables so that rather than propositions such as 'Socrates is a man,' one can have expressions in the form of 'there exists x such that x is Socrates and x is a man,' where 'there exists' is a quantifier while x is a variable. First-order logic can deal with nonlogical objects.

Foundationalism. This concerns philosophical theories of knowledge resting upon justified belief or some secure foundation of certainty, such as a conclusion inferred from a basis of sound premises.

Fruit of the Holy Spirit. This is a biblical term that sums up nine attributes of a person or community living in accord with the Holy Spirit, according to chapter 5 of the epistle to the Galatians: "But the fruit of the Spirit is love, joy, peace, patience, kindness, goodness, faithfulness, gentleness, and self-control."

Fruit of the Holy Spirit (Vulgate Version). The Vulgate version of Galatians lists twelve fruits: charity, joy, peace, patience, benignity (kindness), goodness, longanimity (forbearance), mildness (gentleness), faith, modesty, continency (self-control), and chastity.

Gaslighting. This is a form of psychological manipulation that involves making someone question their own reality, feelings, and experiences of events in order to maintain control over that person.

Guilt-Trip. This is when a person makes someone else feel guilty, especially to induce them to do something.

Heresthetic. This is a political strategy by which a person or group sets or manipulates the context and structure of a decision-making process to win or be more likely to win.

Idealism. This refers to any of various systems of thought in which the objects of knowledge are held to be in some way dependent on the activity of mind.

If-Then Arguments. These are also known as conditional arguments or hypothetical syllogisms and are the workhorses of deductive logic. They make up a loosely defined family of deductive arguments that have an if-then statement—that is, a conditional—as a premise. The conditional has the standard form "if P then Q."

Influence. This is the capacity to have an effect on the character, development, or behavior of someone or something, or the effect itself.

Intermittent Reinforcement (in the context of psychological abuse). This is a pattern of cruel, callous treatment mixed in with random bursts of affection.

Intra-action. This is a Barbadian term used to replace interaction, which necessitates preestablished bodies that then participate in action with each other. Intra-action understands agency as not an inherent property of an individual or human to be exercised but as a dynamism of forces.

Love-Bombing. This is an attempt to influence a person by demonstrations of attention and affection. It can be used in different ways and for either positive or negative purposes. Psychologists have identified love bombing as a possible part of a cycle of abuse and have warned against it. It has also been described as psychological manipulation in order to create a feeling of unity within a group against a society perceived as hostile.

Justification. This is a concept in epistemology used to describe beliefs that one has good reason for holding.

Logic. This is defined as possession of reason, intellectual, dialectical, argumentative. This is also the systematic study of valid rules of inference.

Logical Form. The logical form attempts to formalize a possibly ambiguous statement into a statement with a precise, unambiguous logical interpretation with respect to a formal system.

Manipulate. This means to handle or control (a tool, mechanism, etc.), typically in a skillful manner. It is also defined as to control or influence (a person or situation) cleverly, unfairly, or unscrupulously.

Metaethical. This is the study of the nature, scope, and meaning of moral judgment, which involves second-order or formal questions.

Metaphysical Realism. This is the thesis that the objects, properties, and relations the world contains collectively. It is also defined as the structure of the world (Sider 2011) existing independently of our thoughts about it or our perceptions of it.

Metaphysics. This is the branch of philosophy that deals with the first principles of things, including abstract concepts such as being, knowing, substance, cause, identity, time, and space.

Moral Particularism. This is the claim that there are no defensible moral principles, that moral thought does not consist in the application of moral principles to cases, and that the morally perfect person should not be conceived as the person of principle.

Mysticism. This is any kind of ecstasy or altered state of consciousness that is given a religious or spiritual meaning. It may also refer to the attainment of insight in ultimate or hidden truths and to human transformation supported by various practices and experiences.

Naysayer. This is a person who criticizes, objects to, or opposes something.

Nihilism. This is extreme skepticism maintaining that nothing in the world has a real existence. In the historical sense, this is the doctrine of an extreme Russian revolutionary party (c. 1900), which found nothing to approve of in the established social order.

Normative Ethics. This is the study of the nature, scope, and meaning of moral judgment, which involves first-order or substantive questions.

Operational Model. Operational faith goes beyond just talking about faith to coaching you to live and to operate your life by faith.

Object-Oriented Ontology. This is a twenty-first century Heidegger-influenced school of thought that rejects the privileging of human existence over the existence of nonhuman objects.

Ontology. This is the branch of metaphysics dealing with the nature of being. It is also a set of concepts and categories in a subject area or domain that shows their properties and the relations between them.

Ontologism. This is a philosophical system most associated with Nicolas Malebranche, which maintains that God and divine ideas are the first object of our intelligence and the intuition of God the first act of our intellectual knowledge.

Papal Supremacy. This is the doctrine of the Catholic Church that the pope, by reason of his office as vicar of Christ, the visible source and foundation of the unity both of the bishops and of the whole company of the faithful and as pastor of the entire Catholic Church, has full, supreme, and universal power over the whole Church, a power that he can always exercise unhindered. Briefly, "the pope enjoys, by divine institution, supreme, full, immediate, and universal power in the care of souls."

Passive-Aggressive. The American Psychological Association defines passive-aggressive as "behavior that is seemingly innocuous, accidental, or neutral but that indirectly displays an unconscious aggressive motive."

Passive-Aggressively Posting Online. Passive-aggression, a deliberate but masked way of expressing feelings of anger, is carried out online through such actions as posting embarrassing photos as well as through inactions, such as failing to stop the spread of online gossip.

Philosophical Fallacy. This is a faulty argument, one that is not based on sound reasoning or logic.

Plenary Indulgences. These are certificates believed to reduce the temporal punishment in purgatory for sins committed by the purchasers or their loved ones.

Posteriori Knowledge. This is knowledge that is derived from experienced empirical observation.

Projective Identification. This is a term introduced by Melanie Klein and then widely adopted in psychoanalytic psychotherapy. According to the American Psychological Association, the expression can have two meanings.

> (1) In psychoanalysis, projective identification is a defense mechanism in which the individual projects qualities that are unacceptable to the self onto another person, and that person introjects the projected qualities and believes himself/ herself to be characterized by them appropriately and justifiably.

> (2) In the object relations theory of Melanie Klein, projective identification is a defense mechanism in which a person fantasizes that part of their ego is split off and projected into the object in order to harm or to protect the disavowed part.

Propositional Truths. Truth-functional propositional logic is that branch of propositional logic that limits itself to the study of truth-functional operators. Classical (or "bivalent") truth-functional propositional logic is that branch of truth-functional propositional logic that assumes that there are only two possible truth values a statement (whether simple or complex) can have: (1) truth and (2) falsity, and that every statement is either true or false but not both.

Posteriori. This is a term from logic, which usually refers to reasoning that works backward from an effect to its causes.

Practical Actualization. This is the process of applying self-actualization in a practical manner.

Pragmatism. This is a philosophical tradition that considers words and thought as tools and instruments for prediction, problem-solving, and action and rejects the idea that the function of thought is to describe, represent, or mirror reality.

Prima Scriptura. This is the Christian doctrine that canonized scripture is "first" or "above all" other sources of divine revelation. Implicitly, this view suggests that besides canonical scripture, there can be other guides for what a believer should believe and how they should live, such as the Holy Spirit, created order, traditions, charismatic gifts, mystical insight, angelic visitations, conscience, common sense, the views of experts, the spirit of the times, or something else.

Priori. This is Latin for "from the former."

Priori Knowledge. This is knowledge that is acquired independently of any particular experience.

Proposition. This is defined as the sharable objects of attitudes and the primary bearers of truth and falsity. This means that the term proposition does not refer to particular thoughts or particular utterances (which are not sharable across different instances), nor does it refer to concrete events or facts (which cannot be false).

Propositional Calculus. It deals with propositions (which can be true or false) and relations between propositions, including the construction of arguments based on them.

Propositional Logic. This deals primarily with propositions and logical relations between them.

Protestantism. This is a form of Christianity that originated with the sixteenth century Reformation, a movement against what its followers perceived to be errors in the Catholic Church. They emphasize the priesthood of all believers; justification by faith (sola fide) rather than by good works; the teaching that salvation comes by divine grace or "unmerited favor" only, not as something merited (sola gratia); and either affirm the Bible as being the sole highest authority (sola scriptura "scripture alone") or primary authority (prima scriptura "scripture first") for Christian doctrine rather than being on parity with sacred tradition.

Pseudepigrapha (or Pseudepigraphs). These are falsely attributed works, texts whose claimed author is not the true author, or a work whose real author attributed it to a figure of the past.

Purgatory. According to the belief of some Christian denominations (mostly Catholic), this is an intermediate state after physical death for expiatory purification.

Psychological Manipulation. This is a type of social influence that aims to change the behavior or perception of others through indirect, deceptive, or underhanded tactics.

Rationalism. This is the epistemological view that regards reason as the chief source and test of knowledge.

Realism. This is the attitude or practice of accepting a situation as it is and being prepared to deal with it accordingly.

Redundancies. These are states of being not or no longer needed or useful.

Relativism. This is a family of philosophical views that deny claims to objectivity within a particular domain and assert that facts in that domain are relative to the perspective of an observer or the context in which they are assessed.

Sacrilege. This is the violation or misuse of what is regarded as sacred.

Satisfiability. A formula is satisfiable if it is possible to find an interpretation (model) that makes the formula true.

Satisfiability Modulo Theories. These are decision problems for logical formulas with respect to combinations of background theories expressed in classical first-order logic with equality.

Sectarianism. This is a political or cultural conflict between two groups often related to the form of government they live under.

Self-Actualization. In psychology, this is a concept regarding the process by which an individual reaches his or her full potential.

Septuagint. In the Greek Old Testament, this is the earliest extant Koine Greek translation of books from the Hebrew Bible, various biblical apocrypha, and deuterocanonical books. The first five books of the

Hebrew Bible, known as the Torah or the Pentateuch, were translated in the mid-third century BCE. The remaining books of the Greek Old Testament are presumably translations of the second century BCE.

Seven Gifts of the Holy Spirit. These are an enumeration of seven spiritual gifts originating from patristic authors, later elaborated by five intellectual virtues and four other groups of ethical characteristics. They are as follows: wisdom, understanding, counsel, fortitude, knowledge, piety, and fear of the Lord.

Sola Scriptura. This is a theological doctrine held by some Protestant Christian denominations that posits the Christian scriptures as the sole infallible source of authority for Christian faith and practice.

Solipsism. This is the philosophical idea that only one's mind is sure to exist.

Speculative Realism. This is when something is engaged in, expressing, or based on conjecture rather than knowledge. It is also defined as the quality or fact of representing a person, thing, or situation accurately or in a way that is true to life (a movement in contemporary Continental-inspired philosophy, also known as post-Continental philosophy). It defines itself loosely in its stance of metaphysical realism against its interpretation of the dominant forms of post-Kantian philosophy (or what it terms as "correlationism").

Spiritual Gift/ Charism. This is a concept in Christianity that refers to an endowment or extraordinary power given by the Holy Spirit. These are believed by followers to be supernatural graces that individual Christians need (and needed in the days of the Apostles) to fulfill the mission of the Church. In the narrowest sense, it is a theological term for the extraordinary graces given to individual Christians for the good of others and is distinguished from the graces given for personal sanctification, such as the Seven Gifts of the Holy Spirit and the fruit of the Holy Spirit.

Synthetic Propositions. Truth, if any, derives from how their meaning relates to the world.

Tautology. This is a formula or assertion that is true in every possible interpretation.

Theodicy. It means "vindication of God." It is to answer the question of why a good God permits the manifestation of evil, thus resolving the issue of the problem of evil. Theodicy attempts to provide a framework wherein God's existence is also plausible.

Thirty-Seven Articles. "Thirty-Seven Articles against Corruptions in the Church" is a church reformation declaration against the Catholic Church of England in the late Middle Ages. It had no official title given to it when written, and the author(s) did not identify themselves in the original manuscript. This public declaration by the English medieval sect called the Lollards was announced to the English Parliament at the end of the manifesto Twelve Conclusions of the Lollards published in 1395.

Twelve Conclusions of the Lollards. This is a Middle English religious text containing statements by leaders of the English medieval movement the Lollards inspired by teachings of John Wycliffe. The Conclusions were written in 1395. The text was presented to the Parliament of England and nailed to the doors of Westminster Abbey and St. Paul's Cathedral as a placard (a typical medieval method for publishing). The purpose was to expose what they saw as abuses of the Catholic Church.

Tool Analysis. This helps researchers make sense of the data collected. It enables them to report results and make interpretations.

Transubstantiation. According to the teaching of the Catholic Church, this is "the change of the whole substance of bread into the substance of the Body of Christ and of the whole substance of wine into the substance of the Blood of Christ."

Verbal Abuse. Also known as verbal aggression, verbal attack, verbal violence, verbal assault, psychic aggression, or psychic violence, this is a type of psychological/mental abuse that involves the use of oral, gestured, and written language directed to a victim. Verbal abuse can include the act of harassing, labeling, insulting, scolding, rebuking, or excessive yelling toward an individual. It can also include the use of derogatory terms and the delivery of statements intended to frighten, humiliate, denigrate, or belittle a person. These kinds of attacks may result in mental and/or emotional distress for the victim.

Verificationism. This is also known as the verification principle or the verifiability criterion of meaning. This is the philosophical doctrine that maintains that only statements that are empirically verifiable (i.e., verifiable through the senses) are cognitively meaningful, or else they are truths of logic.

Victim Blaming. Victim blaming occurs when the victim of a crime or any wrongful act is held entirely or partially at fault for the harm that befell them.

Vulgate. It was to become the Catholic Church's officially promulgated Latin version of the Bible during the sixteenth century as the Sixteen Vulgate, then as the Clementine Vulgate. The Vulgate is still presently used in the Latin Church.

Appendices

<u>**Below is a copy of the actual survey taken.**</u>

Terms to Know:

<u>**Metaphysics (Considering Theological Concepts)**</u> is the branch of philosophy that examines the fundamental nature of reality, including the relationship between mind and matter, between substance and attribute, and between potentiality and actuality, dealing with what "is" outside of the physical world with a focus on Souls, Angels, God, Gods and Spirits.

Section A - Participant Demographics

1. **Gender (How do you Identify)**
   __Male __ Female __ Transgender __ Other __ Do not wish to answer

2. **How often do you attend a religious / Spiritual service or gathering?**
   __ 1 once a week ___2'x a week ___ Monthly ____ Holidays ____ Do Not Attend

3. **What are your metaphysical beliefs, do you believe in?**
   ____ God _____ Gods _____ Souls ___ Angels __ Other (write in) _____

4. **Your Religion / Belief**
__ Christian __ Jewish __ Muslim __ Buddhist _____ Other
____ Do not wish to answer

5. **Your Age**
__ Under 18, ___ 18 – 24 ___25-30 __ 31-39 ___ 40-49 ___
50-59 ___ 60-69 ___ 70+

6. **Your level of education:**
____ Below H.S. ___H. S ___ Some College __ Associate ___
Bachelor ____Master ____Ph.D.

7. **Your Income level:**
_____ Below $50,000 _____$50,001 - $ 85,000 _____
$85,001 - $125,000

_____$125,001 - $175,000 _____ $175,000 +

Section B - Instruction: Choose a letter from a-d that best reflects what you think.

1. **What do you consider faith to be?**
   a. Believing in something that you cannot explain
   b. Believing in something that you can explain
   c. A combination of Believing in something that you can & cannot explain
   d. Not Sure

2. **Do you consider yourself faithful?**
   a. Yes
   b. No
   c. Somewhat
   d. Not Sure

3. **What is the basis of your faith?**
   a. Historical religious beliefs alone
   b. Rational religious beliefs alone

c. A combination of both Historical and Rational religion religious beliefs

d. Not Sure

4. **Do you believe that Absolute faith in God is realistic?**

a. Yes

b. No

c. Sometimes

d. Not Sure

5. **Do you believe that your faith can be manipulated by an individual?**

a. Yes

b. No

c. Sometimes

d. Not Sure

6. **Do you believe that your faith can be manipulated by a religious system?**

a. Yes

b. No

c. Sometimes

d. Not Sure

7. **Do you believe that your faith in God can be manipulated by your religious system?**

a. Yes

b. No

c. Sometimes

d. Not Sure

8. **Do you believe that reason and evidence have an impact on your faith in God?**

a. Yes

b. No

c. Sometimes

d. Not Sure

9. **Do you believe that people should have to justify their faith in God?**
   a. Yes
   b. No
   c. Sometimes
   d. Not Sure

Section C - Instruction: From the five- point Likert Scale choose the answer that matches your point of view:

1. **There, has been a breach in the trust placed in faith-based leadership (organized religion)**
   a. Strongly Agree
   b. Agree
   c. Undecided
   d. Disagree
   e. Strongly Disagree

2. **The relationship between metaphysics and religion does impact faith**
   a. Strongly Agree
   b. Agree
   c. Undecided
   d. Disagree
   e. Strongly Disagree

3. **People should have to justify their faith in God.**
   a. Strongly Agree
   b. Agree
   c. Undecided
   d. Disagree
   e. Strongly Disagree

4. **There are exterior factors (out of our realm of physical knowledge) which are really guiding people's thinking and behavior?**
   a. Strongly Agree
   b. Agree
   c. Undecided
   d. Disagree
   e. Strongly Disagree

5. **There is something (Religious impartation) inside of people guiding which is actually guiding people's thinking and behavior?**
   a. Strongly Agree
   b. Agree
   c. Undecided
   d. Disagree
   e. Strongly Disagree

6. **People are autonomous and are not guided by any "Faith Based" system of beliefs.**
   a. Strongly Agree
   b. Agree
   c. Undecided
   d. Disagree
   e. Strongly Disagree

7. **Metaphysics, religion, and faith are connected.**
   a. Strongly Agree
   b. Agree
   c. Undecided
   d. Disagree
   e. Strongly Disagree

Section D - Instruction: Answer true or false. Choose the one that agrees with your point of view concerning "faith."

24	Faith is taught.	True	False
25	Faith is irrational.	True	False
26	Explanations and evidence increase one's faith.	True	False
27	Faith can be explained.	True	False
28	Faith alone is necessary to hold religious beliefs.	True	False
29	Faith alone is necessary to practice religious rites and rituals.	True	False
30	Faith can exist without evidence or explanation.	True	False

REFERENCES

Aczel, Amir D. 2014. *Why Science Does Not Disprove God.* New York: HarperCollins Publishers.

Aquinas, Thomas. (1265–1273) 2006. *Summa Theologiae* vol. 31, "Faith." Translated by T. C. O'Brien. Cambridge: Cambridge University Press.

Arabi, Shahida, MA. 2019. "Narcissists Use Trauma Bonding and Intermittent Reinforcement to Get You Addicted to Them: Why Abuse Survivors Stay." PyschCentral (website). https://psychcentral.com/blog/recovering-narcissist/2019/03/narcissists-use-trauma-bonding-and-intermittent-reinforcement-to-get-you-addicted-to-them-why-abuse-survivors-stay.

Aspin, David N. 2007. *Philosophical Perspectives on Lifelong Learning.* New York: Springer Publishing.

Badke, William B. 2012. *Teaching Research Processes: The Faculty Role in the Development of Skilled Student Researchers.* Oxfordshire, UK: Chandos Publishing. 2018. "When Is Faith Rational?" In *Norton Introduction to Philosophy,* 2nd edition. Edited by Gideon Rosen, Alex Byrne, Joshua Cohen, Elizabeth Harman, and Seana Shiffrin. New York: W. W. Norton, 115–129.

Barad, Karen. 2007. *Meeting the Universe Halfway: Quantum Physics and the Entanglement of Matter and Meaning.* Durham: Duke University Press.

Barnhill, Anne. 2014. "What Is Manipulation?" https://doi.org/10.1093/acprof:oso/9780199338207.003.0003.

Bell, Larry. 2021. "Mystics of Major Historical Importance." Ranker (website). https://www.ranker.com/list/important-mystics-in-history/larry-bell-1.

The Best Schools. n.d. "Daniel Dennett." https://thebestschools.org/features/most-influential-living-philosophers/.

The Best Schools. n.d. "Jaegwon Kim." https://thebestschools.org/features/most-influential-living-philosophers/.

The Best Schools. n.d. "Susan Haack." https://thebestschools.org/features/most-influential-living-philosophers/.

The Best Schools. "William Lane Craig." https://thebestschools.org/features/most-influential-living-philosophers/.

Bishop, John. 1998. "Can There Be Alternative Concepts of God?" *Nous* 32, no. 2 (June): 174–188.
  2002. "Faith as Doxastic Venture." *Religious* Studies 38, no. 4 (December): 471–487.
  2005. "On the Possibility of Doxastic Venture: A Reply to Buckareff." *Religious Studies* 41, no. 4 (December): 447–451.
  2007. *Believing by Faith: An Essay in the Epistemology and Ethics of Religious Belief.* Oxford: Clarendon Press.

Bishop, John, and Ken Perszyk. 2014. "Divine Action beyond the Personal OmniGod." In J. *Oxford Studies in Philosophy of Religion* volume 5, edited by Jonathan L. Kvanvig. Oxford: Oxford University Press, 1–21.

Britannica. n.d. "Epistemology." https://www/britannica.com/topic/epistemology.

California State University, Long Beach. "Thomas Aquinas and the Five Ways." https://web.csulb.edu/~cwallis/100/st2.html.

Chappell, Tim, 1996. "Why Is Faith a Virtue?" *Religious Studies* 32, no. 1 (March): 27–36.

Clegg, J. S. 1979. "Faith." *American Philosophical Quarterly* 16, no. 3 (July): 225–232.

Coyne, Jerry A. 2015. *Faith Versus Fact: Why Science and Religion Are Incompatible.* New York: Viking Press.

Debakcsy, Dale. 2019. "Theano of Croton And the Pythagorean Women of Ancient Greece." https://womenyoushouldknow.net/theano-of-croton-pythagorean/.

Descartes, René. (1641) 1984. "Meditations on First Philosophy." In *Philosophical Writings of Descartes* vol. 2. Translated by John Cottingham, Robert Stoothoff, and Dugald Murdoch. Cambridge: Cambridge University Press, 3–62.

Eddy, Mary Baker. "What Is Christian Science?" Christian Science. Accessed April 24, 2017. http://www.christianscience.com/what-is-christian-science/mary-baker-eddy.

Encyclopedia Britannica. 2021. "Roman Catholicism Summary." *Encyclopedia Britannica.* Accessed September 28, 2022. https://www.britannica.com/summary/Roman-Catholicism.

Exploring Your Mind. 2020. "Victim Blaming Manipulation, a Form of Psychological Violence."https://exploringyourmind.com/victim-blaming-manipulation-psychological- violence/.

Frei, Zsofia. n.d. "Thomas Aquinas and the Rival Process Theology." Academia (website). https://www.academia.edu/1486383/Thomas_Aquinas_and_the_rival_process_theology.

Frei, Zsofia. "Egypt and the Origins of Greek Philosophy."

Gillette, Hope. 2022. "How to Deal with Verbal Abuse." PyschCentral (website). https://psychcentral.com/health/how-to-deal-with-verbal-abuse.

Hall-Flavin, Daniel K. 2021. "What Is Passive-Aggressive Behavior? What Are Some of the Signs?" the Mayo Clinic. https://www.mayoclinic.org/healthy-lifestyle/adult-health/ expert-answers/passive-aggressive-behavior/faq-20057901.

Heil, John. n.d. "The Universe as We Find It." IAI Academy. https://iai.tv/iai-academy/courses/ info?course=the-universe-as-we-find-it.

Heil, John. "John Heil's Lecture on 'Consciousness.'" Phil-Free, uploaded on March 22, 2011, YouTube video, 39:37, https://www.youtube.com/watch?v=-bT3GczeLmY.

Horton, Lindsey. 2019. "The Neuroscience Behind Our Words." BRM Institute. https://brm.institute/neuroscience-behind-words/.

Howard-Snyder, Daniel. 2013. "Schellenberg on Propositional Faith." *Religious Studies* 49, no. 2 (June): 181–194.

Howard-Snyder, Daniel, and Daniel J. McKaughan, 2021. "Faith and Humility: Conflict or Concord?" *Handbook of the Philosophy of Humility*. Edited by Mark Alfano, Michael Lynch, and Alessandra Tanesini. New York: Routledge, 212–224.

Hume, David. (1748) 2007. *An Enquiry Concerning Human Understanding*. Edited by P. Millican. Oxford: Oxford University Press.

Idliby, Ranya, Suzanne Oliver, and Priscilla Warner. 2006. *The Faith Club: A Muslim, A Christian, A Jew—Three Women Search for Understanding*. New York: Atria Imprint of Simon & Schuster, Inc.

Internet Encyclopedia of Philosophy. n.d. "Divine Command Theory." https://iep.utm.edu/divine-c/.

James, William. (1896) 1956. *The Will to Believe, Human Immortality, and Other Essays in Popular Philosophy*. New York: Dover.

Kant, Immanuel. (1787) 1933. *The Critique of Pure Reason,* 2nd edition. Translated by Norman Kemp Smith. London: Macmillan.

Lewis, Rosa B. 1981. "The Philosophical Roots of Lifelong Learning." ERIC. https://eric.ed.gov/?id=ED213356.

Locke, John. (1695) 1999. *The Reasonableness of Christianity: As Delivered in the Scriptures.* Edited by J. C. Higgins-Biddle. Oxford: Clarendon.

Manning, Christel. 2015. *Losing Our Religion: How Unaffiliated Parents Are Raising Their Children.* New York: New York University Press.

McGrath, Alister. 2015. *The Big Question: Why We Can't Stop Talking About Science, Faith and God.* New York: St. Martin's Press.

McKaughan, Daniel J. 2013. "Authentic Faith and Acknowledged Risk: Dissolving the Problem of Faith and Reason." *Religious Studies* 49, no. 1 (March): 101–124.
　　2016. "Action-Centered Faith, Doubt, and Rationality in Advance." *Journal of Philosophical Research* 41: 71–90.

McKaughan, Daniel J., and Daniel Howard-Snyder. 2021. "Theorizing about Faith and Faithfulness with Jonathan Kvanvig." *Religious Studies* 58, no. 3 (September): 628–648.

Metcalfe, Curtis J. 2013. "A Defense of the Kalam Cosmological Argument and the B-Theory of Time." https://irl.umsl.edu/cgi/viewcontent.cgi?article=1186&context=thesis.

Morris, Tom, PhD. 1999. *Philosophy for Dummies.* New York: Wiley Publishing Co.

Moser, Paul K. n.d. "A Posteriori." Routledge Encyclopedia of Philosophy. https://www.rep. routledge.com/articles/thematic/a-posteriori/v-1.

Ni, Preston, MSBA. 2020. "7 Signs of a Passive-Aggressive Gaslighter." Psychology Today (website). https://www.psychologytoday.com/us/blog/communication-success/202010/7-signs-passive-aggressive-gaslighter.

Norwood, Arlisha R. 2017. "Mary Eddy." National Women's History Museum.

Pabst, Adrian. 2012. "Metaphysics: The Creation of Hierarchy." Academia (website). https://www.academia.edu/5481184/ Metaphysics_The_creation_of_hierarchy.

PBS Dramas. "Faith and Reason." https://www.pbs.org/faithandreason/ gengloss/metaph-body. html#:~:text=Derived%20from%20 the%20Greek%20meta,objective%20studies%20of%20 material%20reality.

Philosophy Talk. 2009. "Faith, Reason, and Science." First aired on October 14, 2007. YouTube video. https://www.philosophytalk. org/shows/faith-reason-and-science.

Plantinga, Alvin. 1983. "Reason and Belief in God." In *Faith and Rationality: Reason and Belief in God*. Edited by A. Plantinga and N. Wolterstorff. Notre Dame: University of Notre Dame Press, 16–93.

Pojman, Louis, 1986. "Faith without Belief?" *Faith and Philosophy* 3, no. 2: 157–176.
    2003. "Faith, Doubt and Belief, or Does Faith Entail Belief?" In *The Existence of God*. Edited by R. M. Gale and A. R. Pruss. Aldershot: Ashgate.

Regan, Sarah. 2021. "Are You Manipulative? 13 Behaviors to Watch for in Yourself." MBG Mindfulness. https://www.mindbodygreen. com/articles/am-i-manipulative.

Rudinow, Joel. 1978, "Manipulation." *Ethics* 88, no. 4: 338–347.

Schellenberg, J. L. 1993. *Divine Hiddenness and Human Reason*. Ithaca, NY: Cornell University Press.
    2005. *Prolegomena to a Philosophy of Religion*. Ithaca, NY: Cornell University Press.
    2009. *The Will to Imagine: A Justification of Sceptical Religion*. Ithaca, NY: Cornell University Press.

Seltzer. Leon F. 2014. "Praise as Manipulation: 6 Reasons to Question Compliments." *Psychology Today*.https://www. psychologytoday.com/us/blog/evolution-the-self /201401/ praise-manipulation-6-reasons-question-compliments.

Shuavarnnasri, Jayda, MA. "What Is Gaslighting? How to Know If You're Experiencing It in a Relationship." MBG Relationships.https://www.mindbodygreen.com/articles/ signs-of- gaslighting-in-relationships.

Simone Marie. 2022. "Why the 'Guilt Trip' Comes Naturally (but Can Be Problematic)." PsychCentral (website). https://psychcentral. com/health/guilt-trip#is-it-toxic.

Smith, Wilfred Cantwell. 1979. *Faith and Belief*. Princeton: Princeton University Press.

Stanford Encyclopedia of Philosophy. (1996) 2019. "Ontological Arguments." https://plato.stanford.edu/entries/ ontological-arguments/.

Study.com. n.d. "The Cosmological Principle." Audio-Video Presentation, 5:29. study.com/academy/lesson/the-cosmological-principle.html.

Teaching American History. "Jonathan Edwards: American Minds." Podcast Ep. 501. https://teachingamericanhistory.org/blog/ meet-jonathan-edwards/.

TruthUnity. n.d. "Metaphysical Meaning of Faith (RW)." https://www. truthunity.net/rw/faith.

WebMD Editorial Contributors. 2023. "Manipulation: Symptoms to Look For." https://www.webmd.com/mental-health/ signs-manipulation.

Wikibooks. n.d. "Hebrew Roots/The Original Foundation / Faith." https://en.wikibooks.org/wiki/Hebrew_Roots/The_original_ foundation/Faith.

Wikipedia. n.d. "Fact-Value Distinction." https://en.wikipedia.org/
wiki/Fact%E2%80%93value_distinction#David_Hume's_
skepticism

Wikipedia. n.d. "Logical Positivism." https://en.wikipedia.org/wiki/
Logical_positivism.

Wikipedia. n.d. "Manipulation (Psychology)." https://en.wikipedia.
org/wiki/Manipulation_(psychology)#:~:text=Feigning%20
innocence%3A%20Manipulator%20tries%20to,and%20
possibly%20their%20own%20sanity.

Wireless Philosophy. "PHILOSOPHY - Religion: Cosmological
Argument #1." YouTube video, 7:44. https://www.youtube.com/
watch?v=2zS1HiuWPMA. https://www.ukessays.com/essays/
philosophy/the-anselm-ontological-argument-philosophy-
essay.php

ABOUT THE AUTHOR

Dr. Kim Spivey-Hunter is a seasoned motivator, educator, and Christian counselor that's deeply immersed in the sea of spiritual exploration. Guided by her Christian faith, her experiences and insightful conversations with various church leaders and members have fueled her commitment to understanding her holistic place within the Christian faith.

Motivated by a quest for scriptural clarity amidst diverse perspectives, Dr. Kim has undertaken a comprehensive study of manipulation. Recognizing that individual experiences may not always align with scriptural principles, she is devoted to ensuring that, as a Christian counselor, her guidance remains firmly grounded in the scriptures. Her mission is clear – to provide individuals with the scriptural foundation for success in life, untethered by personal interpretations.

Dr. Kim's unique blend of motivation, education, and Christian counseling sets her apart as a compassionate guide in navigating the complexities of faith. Through her work, she seeks to empower individuals to an intellectual odyssey, inviting them to discover their own spiritual journey, free from the influence of external conditions. Dr. Kim Spivey-Hunter is more than an author; she is a dedicated advocate for scriptural authenticity and holistic well-being.

To contact Dr. Kim Spivey-Hunter, please email her:
kimskloset01@gmail.com

www.ingramcontent.com/pod-product-compliance
Lightning Source LLC
Chambersburg PA
CBHW052114030426
42335CB00025B/2979